VOLUNTEERS FOR TODAY'S CHURCH

VOLUNTEERS FOR TODAY'S CHURCH

How to Recruit and Retain Workers

DENNIS E. WILLIAMS & KENNETH O. GANGEL

Baker Books

A Division of Baker Book House Co
Grand Rapids, Michigan 49516

© 1993 by Dennis E. Williams and Kenneth O. Gangel

Published by Baker Books
a division of Baker Book House Company
P.O. Box 6287, Grand Rapids, MI 49516-6287

Printed in the United States of America

Library of Congress Cataloging-in-Publication Data

Gangel, Kenneth O.
    Volunteers for today's church: how to recruit and retain workers
/ Kenneth O. Gangel and Dennis E. Williams.
       p. cm.
    Includes bibliographical references.
    ISBN 0-8010-3861-8
    1. Lay ministry. 2. Lay ministry—Recruiting. I. Williams,
Dennis E. II. title.
BV677.G36 1993
253′.7—dc20
                                           93-10370

Contents

89086

Introduction

The Christian education board members arrived for the specially called meeting feeling uneasy, since last month had found only the chairperson and the minister of education present. The report on the fall program came as a shock to some. Even this late in August there were still serious staff needs, especially for the Sunday school and the weekday boys' and girls' clubs. Church leaders also planned to begin a third worship service at 8:00 A.M. and, of course, wanted an additional children's program during that hour. Even though only children from birth through age five would have a program at 8:00 o'clock, it would still require extensive recruiting and training of several new workers.

Actually it was a struggle to staff the 9:30 A.M. Sunday school, the 11:00 A.M. children's church, and the Wednesday evening boys' and girls' programs. Work on a new 8:00 A.M. staff added to the already difficult recruitment pressures.

One member of the board said she did not realize the church had such a serious worker shortage. When she heard the report from the Sunday school superintendent on the list of needed workers, she was amazed. Perhaps also the rest of the church was unaware. They had made announcements, but with practically no response. In fact, some programs had been canceled for the summer, primarily because of too few workers.

Certainly there must be a balance between constantly asking for volunteers and keeping the church informed about basic worker needs. No crisis appeared imminent, but the situation presented a serious challenge.

Board members concluded that a church their size (800 in attendance) must house a lot of spectators with very few actually serving in a ministry. There were no records, however, to substantiate this hunch.

One member suggested they needed an up-to-date inventory of the membership to identify potential workers. Another said that a survey had been completed a few years ago and the information was in the office. The minister of education pronounced those data out-of-date and not useful.

Sound familiar? This type of dilemma, centering around the recruitment of volunteers, goes on weekly in churches across the land. It is not limited by size, location, or type of church. Nor is this book so limited. The issues involved in volunteer recruitment, training, and retention are common to churches from 50 to 5000.

The 1990s bring unique pressures to churches trying to staff their programs with volunteers. Today's society consumes more of people's time through extra jobs, recreation, and family pressures. Priorities different from and opposed to biblical standards indicate spiritual problems.

All of this underscores the results of a 1988 survey given to 790 Christian education practitioners with 90.8 percent of the sample in full-time ministry. The most difficult issue they anticipate in church education ministries during this decade is frustrated attempts to recruit people for ministry.[1]

Regardless of the reasons given, the problem looms both real and acute. Churches today are expected to have full ministry programs to reach new people and minister to present members. If they don't, people will go to a church that does.

How do churches accomplish the seemingly impossible task of staffing church programs with volunteer workers, when these workers are so hard to find, enlist, and train? This book provides a biblical and realistic strategy for recruitment. And we have directed our ideas at the entire arena of church leadership—professional and lay. We think senior pastors in multiple staff churches need this information, but so do struggling departmental superintendents or the chairperson of an evangelization committee.

Don't expect a quick fix. Perhaps churches experience the results of poor planning in the past. Many churches operate in crisis management. When they need workers, they merely fill the positions without regard to proper enlistment, training, orientation, and supervision. This often results in volunteers serving a limited time, making it necessary to find others as the cycle repeats itself.

Every church needs a strategy of recruitment, from a biblical understanding of volunteer ministry to the retention of people in service. Too many churches still place people in positions and hope for the best. Evangelical congregations must approach the task armed with a philosophy of ministry that honors the work of the Lord and allows people to be fulfilled in ministry. No longer can they merely run programs; they must help people develop their spiritual gifts and be sensitive to a mutual ministry to and in the body. Only ministry developed from real needs will attract church support through prayer, finances, and volunteer staffing.

God's people must be involved in biblical ministry that is mutually developed, based on needs, and assists people to experience God's blessing in their service for him. This approach can dramatically reduce the number of spectators in the congregation.

One solution to the crisis in volunteers is to have more people serve with smaller time commitments. If, as suggested by authors in the field, a small percentage of a congregation does most of the work, churches should try to increase this percentage by spreading the work load around. And not just on paper. People need to understand their ministries and be supervised to see them accomplished. Delegation and evaluation both have a place in the development of lay leaders. Neither should be overlooked, or the results will be less than satisfactory.

Do not forget the needs of folks presently serving. Are they overworked? Exhausted? In need of a break? By balancing work loads the church can help them do a better job with fewer responsibilities, and they will feel better about their service to the Lord.

Look beyond the few who presently serve to the many who attend church but do not contribute their time and effort. This is the pool of potential servants you need to penetrate. They need to be approached prayerfully, challenged to serve, and offered training and assistance in their new tasks. They need the fulfillment that comes from serving the Lord.

At the end of each chapter you will find a series of questions or activities to help you apply the content to your church situation. Working through these activities will help you develop a strategy for team ministry based on biblical principles.

One more thought. We want to express public thanks to Christy Sullivan and Ginny Murray, who worked closely with us in the preparation of this manuscript.

1

Understanding Biblical
Lay Leadership

Every February, First Church pulls its international flags out of the closets, dusts off the *Foods of the World* cookbook, and gets ready for the annual missionary conference. Count on it; sometime during that week a speaker or two will deliver a message from Matthew 9:35–38. Like the Great Commission of Matthew 28, evangelicals accept as commonplace, perhaps even mandatory, an interpretation of such passages which form the foundation for global evangelism. But let's review the context.

As Jesus went through the towns and villages, he pointed out to the disciples the condition of the people. He called them harassed and helpless sheep without a shepherd. He said, "The harvest is plentiful but the workers are few. Ask the Lord of the harvest, therefore, to send out workers into his harvest field"

(Matt. 9:37–38). What exactly is the "harvest field"? Global missions? That fits, of course, but the passage also applies to volunteer positions in the church. Although the Lord simply asks the Christian to pray that people will be sent into the harvest, presumably that prayer implies a willingness to become one of those workers.

Nature and Purpose of the Church

What does the Bible say about the mission of the church? Only if we understand its purpose can we write objectives that reflect the biblical message. Those objectives allow the church to see how well it fulfills Matthew 28. Areas of need will surface and we can set goals to treat them. When a need-meeting purpose, clear objectives, and specific goals have been established, we can develop plans for reaching our goals. A congregation that has adopted realistic strategies for ministry stands ready to deal with the struggles of this tempestuous decade.

Mission Statement

Where do we find information on the purpose of the church? Perhaps it is necessary to know how Jesus' disciples implemented his commission. The significant passage in Acts 2:41–47 provides a good glimpse. Here are some of the activities of the early church. They evangelized, baptized, learned doctrine from the apostles, fellowshiped, broke bread, prayed, saw signs and wonders, shared their belongings, gave to anyone who had need, met in the temple courts, ate meals together in homes, and praised God.

These activities can be divided into the categories of worship, evangelism, education, fellowship, and ministry. Worship included baptism, the Lord's Supper, prayer, and praise. Evangelism resulted in people accepting the gospel message. Education occurred as the believers devoted themselves to the apostles' teaching. Fellowship took place through meeting and eating. Ministry describes how Christians met the needs of others.

This outline can help identify a mission statement: The purpose of a church is to be a worshiping fellowship engaged in evangelism, education, and ministry—the body of Christ in an alien world.

Each worshiping fellowship has one thing in common as it engages in evangelism, education, and ministry: the recognition that Jesus Christ is the head of the body, the church (Col. 1:18). As the focus in this book is on the recruitment and retention of leaders, note that the goals and objectives tie into the relationship of the people to the Lord. This relationship is direct, not mediated by others; Christ alone is that mediator, the goal of worship and service (Heb. 9:15). Paul Stevens gives this reminder:

> No church leader in the New Testament is even ever called the head of a local body. That title is reserved for Jesus. The head does not tell the hand to tell the foot what to do. The head is connected directly with the foot. Therefore people find their ministries not by being directed by the leaders but by being motivated and equipped and directed by the Head himself. . . . In other words, the church is not a hierarchy but a monarchy. The will of the Head is not mediated through various levels of government (pastors, elders or deacons, small group leaders and so on), but comes directly to all his subjects.[1]

A church develops its personal mission statement from its understanding of both the universal and local purpose for its fellowship. This mission statement then brings purpose and meaning to ministry. People will be more motivated to serve as they can see why the church carries out its various ministries.

Identifying Objectives

From the mission statement a church can write several objectives that will lead to fulfillment of its purpose. Objectives need not be measured specifically; goals face that scrutiny. But objectives do identify the kinds of ministry we consider important. In general these include worship, evangelism, education, fellowship, and ministry. To be a bit more specific, we can write objectives for each of these five areas. But remember, churches must identify objectives that clearly communicate to the congregation why they perform certain ministries.

Discovering Needs

When its purpose has been established, a church should seek to discover what needs God has raised for it to meet in the neighborhood, community, county, state, nation, and world and then evaluate itself as to how it meets those needs. Such evaluation threatens some, but remember that evaluation seeks improvement, not punishment or reprimand.

Consider *worship*. Everyone agrees on its importance. But how well does your church do it? Do the people sense the presence of God in their services? Do they communicate with God? What about the style? What about the music? Is the Word of God proclaimed? People have different tastes, but quality control and biblical allegiance are both important in the way they approach God.

Evangelism may seem easier to measure, but merely counting the number of people coming to Christ in a given year may not offer a complete evaluation. Are those converts growing in Christ through the ministry of the church? Do parishioners give regular testimony for Christ to their friends, neighbors, and business acquaintances? Do they give evangelism proper emphasis in the total ministry of the church?

Education usually focuses on Sunday school ministry. Not all education in the church takes place on Sunday morning, but Sunday school certainly is the largest program involving the most people. Other opportunities such as Bible studies, fellowship groups, and special studies can be included. How effective is the curriculum plan? Are the various studies coordinated to avoid overlap and/or omission of important content? Is the learning relevant and practical or merely factually oriented? Are lives obviously changed through the teaching of the Word? What help do the teachers need to improve the educational ministry?

Fellowship seems too informal to evaluate. But several questions do surface. Does the church have a spirit of fellowship? Does the church promote fellowship opportunities? Usually this cannot be done in a large group. Many churches develop small-group ministries to provide closer relationships among their members.

Finally, consider *ministry needs*. People in every congregation have needs, though they may be hesitant to reveal them. How can the church discover people who have needs? By looking all around. One adult Sunday school leader stood before his class a couple of weeks before Thanksgiving and stated with excitement that he had "found" a poor family. He encouraged the class to bring food to prepare a basket for these needy folks. Yet many more needy people lived across the street from the church. Most churches need not "find" poor people; sometimes they even attend church classes. The economic changes of the 1990s have caused some people to lose their jobs and other resources. They may be reluctant to admit the problem, but God wants Christians to identify such people and help them (Acts 4:32–35).

Setting Goals

As needs are discovered, they can be organized under suggested ministry categories. Specific goals can be set to meet some of those needs. It will be impossible to address every need discovered, so needs must be prioritized with work begun on those most pressing. Others will have to wait until later.

Goals should take the form of specific, measurable statements. This way we can carefully evaluate them. For example, if we state that we want to have all of our Sunday school teachers attend at least one special training seminar in the next twelve months, it would be quite easy to see how well we achieve that. Not all goals are that easy to write out, but give it a try. Write statements that can be measured.

Finally, all of this can be brought together into an overall strategy for the ministry of the local church. In it you will have identified (1) your purpose for ministry, (2) how you will measure needs, (3) how well you are achieving your objectives, (4) what ministry areas you want to prioritize, (5) what strategies will help you reach your goals, and (6) how to organize the total ministry of the church.

With this in hand, you can recruit volunteers by explaining how an available service post fits into the total ministry of the church. A church often enlists people to fill a position; it should enlist them to serve Christ through his body.

Spiritual Service

The word *service* is in both the Old and New Testaments, where it shows that God considers all his people servants. How did Bible characters understand spiritual service? What does it mean to believers today?

Remember the disciples' quarrel recorded in Mark 10? The Lord scolded them for ambition and said, "Whoever wants to become great among you must be your servant, and whoever wants to be first must be slave of all. For even the Son of Man did not come to be served, but to serve, and to give his life as a ransom for many" (Mark 10:43–45). He also demonstrated it by washing their feet, a job reserved for the lowest servant in the household. In Philippians 2 the apostle Paul reminds Christians how the Lord took on the form of a servant. Earlier in the chapter he instructs them to avoid selfish ambition and, in humility, consider others better than themselves.

Biblical Servanthood

But servanthood hardly seems a popular topic today. Jesus reversed the common understanding of leadership by teaching and demonstrating humility and service in a most profound way. His example is essential to an understanding of how church ministry must be carried out. Grandiose concepts of leaders who control others run counter to an understanding of spiritual service. Of course, churches do house both leaders and followers; the real issue deals with the attitude and purpose of leaders and how they serve their followers in the congregation.

All believers can be involved in some form of spiritual service. Peter calls us to use our gifts to serve others (1 Peter 4:10). He admonishes the chosen people of God to offer spiritual sacrifices acceptable to God through Jesus Christ (1 Peter 2:4–5). Certainly *acceptable* means that the servants should give their best from the resources given them by God—possessions, relationships, position, education, experiences, opportunities, abilities, and gifts. The parables provide illustrations of how believers can be good stewards of these resources.

The Bible teaches that believers should discharge their service to the best of their ability, both inside and outside the church. God requires some form of service from his people, and to neglect it is contrary to his design. According to George Barna, the church can establish a pool of volunteers by helping people realize the practical meaning of the New Testament's teaching about servanthood and their responsibilities as followers of Christ. Ministry is a give-and-take proposition.[2]

A study of the use of spiritual gifts in ministry helps the church understand God's plan for the utilization of its people in ministry. Key passages include Romans 12, 1 Corinthians 12–14, Ephesians 4:11–16, and 1 Peter 2. The gifted people listed in Ephesians include apostles, prophets, evangelists, pastors, and teachers. And the purpose of these specific gifts seems to encompass all Christians: "To prepare God's people for works of service, so that the body of Christ may be built up until we all reach unity in the faith and in the knowledge of the Son of God and become mature, attaining to the whole measure of the fullness of Christ" (Eph. 4:12–13).

Clearly the professional staff should *not* do all the work of ministry. They must equip and train God's people to serve. Someone has said that over 90 percent of the church training dollar goes into the training of the clergy. What about the importance of training all the Lord's people for service? We do not suggest that churches should not hire professional staff to lead them in their ministry. Rather, we emphasize that the professional staff must provide the leadership that equips and trains all of God's people for some kind of service.

When professionals take over the ministry, they keep other people whom God has gifted from serving. Two problems result. The professional staff will be overworked because they do not share the load. And people will become either bitter or indifferent to the church if they do not have an opportunity to serve and use the gifts God has given them. George Gallup, Jr., states:

> To a growing extent, survey evidence indicates, the Church of the future will be shaped from the "bottom up" rather than the "top down." And so it becomes increasingly important to give the laity a voice in the leadership of churches. In one survey we discovered that Americans by a 6-to-1 ratio said the laity (the people who attend religious services) should have greater influence in their churches. The ratio is yet higher among young upscale groups, who will provide a large share of the leadership of churches in the future.[3]

Essential Training

Often we hear the statement, "Good teachers will train people to do the work and eventually work themselves out of a job." Although this cliché carries some truth, it needs clarification. Yes, we must train and equip people to do the work of ministry and, as far as possible, let them have freedom to grow and develop. This does not mean however, that leaders have nothing left to do. Wise leaders discover other areas of ministry so they can repeat the process by training and equipping others to take over new ministries.

Certain aspects of ministry require professional attention on a continuing basis, but even in these areas it is essential to train others. Some missionaries seem to understand this concept better. They go to a field and, at first, do most of the work. Then, after they have gathered a group of converts, they train those people to do the work and the missionaries move on to repeat the process with another group. Though training will be discussed later, here we must underscore the importance of leaders not only discovering spiritual gifts but also developing them.

Several years ago a well-known evangelist talked about his first attempt at witnessing. If you knew this person and his ministry, you would readily admit that he has the gift of evangelism, and God has used him remarkably in this way. But his first witnessing encounter was hardly polished. In fact, his audience laughed at his description of it. He had seemed to say and do everything wrong. What happened? Had God not gifted him in evangelism? The gift was there all right, but he needed to develop it. He did just that, and over the years he has become an effective evangelist.

Some people try to assess people's spiritual gifts and then place them in positions of service. Sounds good, right? But most of the time gifts surface in the context of ministry. How do you find a person with the gift of teaching? You watch that person teach and then see if God confirms the gift by results. Spiritual-gifts inventories may be helpful, but they are only one means of assessment. Experiments in ministry demonstrate gifts; effective leaders devote time to developing them.

Philosophy of Recruitment

Today churches seem to struggle with both the quantity and the quality of workers. Yet, every congregation contains the necessary potential workers or trained leadership to meet the needs of that particular group of Christians. Such cheery optimism will seem ill-founded to those struggling with service vacancies. We can hear the complaint: "You don't understand our situation."

But we do not claim that you have enough people to serve every possible *program* of the church, only enough to meet the leadership needs. Too many church programs seem to have little or nothing to do with current needs, and, perhaps, should not survive.

Effective churches minister in ways they feel God calls them to; they try to do a few things well. When they overextend their ministries, they place undue pressure on the entire congregation. A fine balance exists between giving people a challenge and asking them to do too much. *Since Jesus Christ is Lord of the church, and the Holy Spirit gives gifts to the church's people to fulfill works of ministry, God will call into his service the people necessary to meet its essential needs.*

So what happens when you cannot find the needed workers? Perhaps it is time to evaluate the ministry. Leaders must be sensitive enough to recognize that it might be necessary to table, or eliminate, a certain program or ministry until the right people share the burden to make it work.

First Church conducted an effective Wednesday night boys' club program. For several years the program served the boys of the church and brought in others from the neighborhood. One year as fall approached, several of the previous workers had either moved away or felt they could no longer serve, so the program was not fully staffed. People prayed, made phone calls and announcements, planned training sessions, but still there were not enough workers.

Finally the congregation decided that perhaps the Lord wanted them to put this important program on hold until they could find the necessary people. They went an entire year without this valuable ministry, but the church did not collapse, the pastor was not fired, no one asked for a recall of the board; instead, the ministry of the church continued. In time, enough workers were found and trained and the following fall they reinstated the program.

Why do people feel that all programs they operate must continue forever? Why call anything "First Annual"? Why make a currently good idea something that future generations will have to follow? Some ministries can be one-time events, and the effectiveness of other ministries can determine their longevity.

However, the problem of discovering workers looms much larger than having too many programs. In the next chapter we will address the question of why churches experience a shortage of workers. Lack of spiritual commitment on the part of some of the Lord's people poses a genuine threat to contemporary evangelicalism. Surely one reason for the shortage of workers stems from improper priorities and a mistaken understanding of life as divided into "secular" and "sacred" roles. In Western societies people tend to divide their lives into the different roles they play, with vocation being work but spiritual calling something quite different. The obvious results: no longer a group of people intimately fitted together as one body, but a group of independent individuals working part-time at being the church.[4]

Perhaps a larger percentage of people are not involved in church ministry because they have not been taught to understand the true nature of the church. Church leaders must understand this lack and work to overcome it. We must reverse the "too-much-on-too-few" syndrome; it leads to burnout and ineffective ministry. The alternative is to share leadership with others who will feel a part of the total ministry and be fulfilled in serving the Lord.

Recognition for successful ministries goes to the Lord and to *all* the people involved, not just to the one person heading up a program. It takes a team effort with people working together to do the work of the Lord. Our society focuses on individuals and leaders, but a leader's success depends on his or her followers. Wise leaders usually say, "I could not have done it without the help of others," and they are absolutely right. Christian leaders do not work for the accolades of others but for the words of our Lord: "Well done, good and faithful servant."

This puts the work of ministry in perspective. When difficulties come (and they certainly will) we go back to the purpose of service to determine our motives. Sure, we can recruit people using personal appeal with incorrect motives. (We may be so desperate to find workers that we do it all the time.) But the results will be destructive and counterproductive. Be open and honest. Try to find workers the Lord has called to serve, rather than use a shortcut that produces chaos and is a detriment to the ministry. Go back to the biblical pattern and to the personalized approaches. Allow God's Spirit to call forth his people into the necessary ministry posts, those harvest fields waiting for workers.

Application Activities

1. From Scripture, discover the purpose of your church and write objectives for each of the broad areas.

2. Look at your church's constitution and/or bylaws to see what its founders identified as a purpose statement. Compare this statement with what you learned from the scriptural study.

3. Evaluate how well the church is doing in reaching the objectives.

4. What areas of need arise from this evaluation? List them under the categories of worship, evangelism, education, fellowship, and service.

5. Set a list of priorities related to the needs you identified and set goals to meet the needs.

6. Using the above five categories of needs, list the possible strategies to reach the goals under each category and work out a ministry calendar for one year.

7. Discuss the concept of spiritual service as presented in this chapter. What is it? Where is it taught? What does it mean to say that everyone should have some place of service? How can this concept be communicated effectively to the staff and the congregation?

8. How does the concept of spiritual gifts assist the congregation to do the work of ministry? Why is it important to do more than merely discover the spiritual gifts?

9. What is the traditional relationship of the clergy and the laity with regard to ministry? What problems

can arise from a misunderstanding of this concept? What is the biblical role of the clergy in relationship to the laity?

10. How can churches build a team concept of ministry?

 **2**

Problems in Recruitment

L inda, Women's Ministry has a need for someone to coordinate all the luncheons and refreshments for the weekly meetings. I know you are good at that sort of thing. Will you give it a try?"

"No; thanks, anyway. I don't think I want to do anything this year. The children's sports activities are going to keep me busy, and I'm going to work at the school one day a week as well."

The recruiter walked away from this meeting deeply troubled by the response to her request. Not that Linda's excuses weren't legitimate. Her children were talented athletes, and they played on a number of local teams. In addition, the elementary school needed volunteers almost as much as the church. But the recruiter knew Linda well, knew that she was a highly energetic woman, a Christian unquestionably, but one who chose not to give her talents and time to the church. She also knew that Linda had at one time shown much greater interest.

After she filled the position with another volunteer, the recruiter went back to Linda to gain more insight. Linda's response was enlightening.

"I really don't feel needed by the church. I'm not a college graduate; I'm not rich; I'm just an ordinary person. On top of that, I've been divorced and feel like a lot of people in the church look down on me for that. I don't know the Bible very well, but most of the time what they want is a Sunday school teacher.

"Yes, I was more involved in my church before we moved here. They didn't seem to ask more of me than I could give and acted very glad to have me around. Very simply, I don't feel loved and cared for. I stay because my children have friends here."

A sad but wiser recruiter left the meeting, knowing that she had witnessed a two-way failure here—both Linda and the church failing to serve each other.

If a problem well defined is half solved, we need to define the many struggles connected with the recruitment of volunteers for ministry. Though it may not be possible to solve all the problems we discuss, we can certainly understand them better.

Spiritual Problems

On the surface, it looks as though the majority of church members do not have a commitment to the work of the church. Often it has been said that the vast majority of the work of the church is done by a small percentage of the membership, while the rest merely attend services. Obviously, many laypersons remain uncommitted to church work, or at least that seems to be one logical conclusion.

Lack of Commitment

On a deeper level, it may not be quite that clear-cut. Many of the noninvolved may themselves be the recipients of ministry. In one small church over a period of three years, three men were struck down with terminal illnesses, all in their prime years, leaving three widows and several fatherless children. The *work* of that church did seem to suffer during that time, but the *ministry* of the church moved forward powerfully. Many people prepared meals, cleaned houses, ran errands, took care of financial matters, helped with funeral arrangements, provided compassionate listening ears, and spent time with hurting children.

Furthermore, all church rolls contain lists of members who need to be out of active ministry for a while. Our Lord gave one day in seven for rest and provided for the land to rest one year in seven. So can volunteers use time away for refreshment and renewal. In addition, many church members may have volunteer commitments that are not connected with the local church but have great effect on the worldwide body of Christ.

Nonetheless, some need a greater challenge to take up active service in the church. To do this without incurring legalistic obligation, the pastoral staff would be well advised to think through their own leadership roles.

Lack of Leadership

Eugene Habecker speaks insightfully of the spiritual qualifications of a leader, suggesting that "a person's walk with God is always seen as indispensable for a leadership assignment."[1] While Habecker notes that the Old Testament is filled with leaders chosen at

God's own discretion, certain qualifications do appear for leadership:

1. God looks for leaders who have hearts perfect toward Him.
2. God looks for leaders of great inner spiritual stature.
3. What God expects of leaders He also desires for all of us.[2]

Habecker also notes three significant New Testament cautions aimed at leaders:

1. Don't seek to be first.
2. Prefer others.
3. Don't lord your leadership over others.[3]

What is the primary goal of God-given leaders in the church? Ephesians states it clearly:

It was he who gave some to be apostles, some to be prophets, some to be evangelists, and some to be pastors and teachers, to prepare God's people for works of service, so that the body of Christ may be built up until we all reach unity in the faith and in the knowledge of the Son of God and become mature, attaining to the whole measure of the fullness of Christ (Eph. 4:11–13).

Paul Stevens has written this:

First, church leadership is called *primarily* to an equipping ministry. This is not a sideline to preaching or counseling, but the raison d'etre of the pastor-teacher. Second, equipping the saints does not mean harnessing the laity for the felt needs or institutional tasks of the church nor harnessing the laity to assist the pastor with certain delegated ministries. The saints are to be equipped *for their own ministry.* The pastor should not be trying to replicate his or her own ministry but to release theirs. In the process, the laity, as a separate category of ministry in the body of Christ, is abolished.[4]

When we have a clear and working definition of New Testament leadership, and leaders committed to that definition, then we may move on to ask for a commitment of service from our church members. The following sums up New Testament leadership principles:

1. Leadership is ministry. The emphasis on service and the thrust of the gift of leadership in Romans 12:8 shows us that if New Testament leadership means anything, it means serving other people. With meekness church leaders involve themselves in concert with other believers to engage in ministry. The smog of selfishness and egoism lifts to make mutual ministry a biblical reality.

2. Leadership is modeling behavior. We can see it clearly in the Paul and Timothy relationship (1 Tim. 4:11–16; 2 Tim. 3:10–15). Lawrence O. Richards says it well: "The spiritual leader who is a servant does not demand. He serves. In his service the spiritual leader sets an example for the body—an example that has compelling power to motivate heart change."[5]

3. Leadership is membership in the body. Obviously this does not refer to the placement of one's name on the roll, but rather the identification of the leader with all other congregants. In Romans 12:4–5 Paul writes, "Just as each of us has one body with many members . . . so in Christ we who are many form one body, and each member belongs to all the others." The issue of relating to other people is inseparable from an under-

standing of Christian leadership, the measure of which can only be shown when the leader serves the body in meekness and membership.[6]

When people join a church, we may take the opportunity to teach them how they can be involved in service. As we present various opportunities and enlist these people in some form of ministry, we should carefully follow the Spirit's leading. People can be challenged to find just the right place of service in which they can both be fulfilled and contribute to the ministry of the church.

When people choose not to serve, church leaders do well to seek an understanding of the reasons. Many have too many commitments in other areas, while some just show no interest in serving. Perhaps both need to be challenged from a spiritual perspective.

Watching how people invest their time and resources helps us know what they feel is important. This is what motivates them. Then we may challenge these people to identify and adopt biblical priorities which will bring spiritual fulfillment and satisfaction.

Lack of Leaders' Prayers

Even when church leaders devote themselves to a servant mentality and are careful to present challenges for service, they still may find themselves short of volunteers. Then is the time to focus on the need for prayer to undergird the volunteer ministry.

A seminary class topic one day centered on recruitment. Using brainstorming, the students suggested ways the church could recruit workers. They filled the chalkboard with ideas and suggestions. Suddenly someone from the back of the room raised his hand and suggested prayer. The class fell silent. Then they realized what they had done, or rather what they had not done. They had minimized the need for prayer by suggesting it last. The biblical pattern calls leaders to pray first, seeking God's help in finding people to serve. One of the students, a children's pastor, told of his desperate need for workers. The class spent special time in prayer for him and for his ministry. The next week he came to class and reported that several people had actually called him to volunteer.

We want to be sure this book does not extend the error of neglecting prayer. Readers should not overlook the importance of prayer and jump right into the many suggestions for getting people involved in ministry. Without the guidance of the Holy Spirit, which comes as a result of sincere prayer, our efforts in finding necessary workers will be limited to our own strength and ideas. It is the Lord's church, and we serve him.

As we pray, remember that we are not merely seeking to fill positions; we want to equip people for mature service. At the beginning of the chapter, we told about Linda and her sense of feeling unneeded and unimportant to church leaders. The church failed Linda, not because she was not plugged into some appropriate service, but because she herself did not feel adequately cared for and so did not feel the freedom to care for others. Eugene Peterson expresses some unique observations on the nature of the type of pastoral ministry you need:

> The Reformers recovered the biblical doctrine of justification by faith. . . . The vocational reformation of our own time (if it turns out to be that) is a rediscovery of the pastoral work of the cure of souls. The phrase sounds antique. It is antique. But it is not obsolete. It catches up and coordinates, better than any other expression I am aware of, the unending warfare against

sin and sorrow and the diligent cultivation of grace and faith to which the best pastors have consecrated themselves in every generation. . . . The cure of souls is a cultivated awareness that God has already seized the initiative. The traditional doctrine defining this truth is prevenience: God everywhere and always seizing the initiative. He gets things going. He had and continues to have the first word. Prevenience is the conviction that God has been working diligently, redemptively, and strategically before I appeared on the scene, before I was aware there was something here for me to do.[7]

Some years ago a family visited the Williams household for a weekend. When they were prepared to leave, their car would not start. Immediately they prayed, asking God to repair their car and make it start. After waiting for several hours, someone suggested that it might be a good idea to have a mechanic look at the car and repair it. Finally they agreed, and went on their way later that afternoon. Why didn't God repair the car? Certainly he was able, but for reasons known only to him he chose not to. Furthermore, the availability of mechanical skill represents God's common grace.

Some church leaders approach recruitment much like those friends dealt with car repair. When their churches need personnel in various educational programs, they pray and wait for people who see the need to volunteer. As you can guess, few come forward. Eventually other workers resign because of overwork and lack of support or help from the staff. Do not overlook the importance of prayer; do not overlook the importance of what we can contribute to meet the need.

Administrative Problems

Some folks have difficulty using the word *administration* in a church setting. They feel that implementing "secular business techniques" in the church departs from the scriptural pattern. But notice that the word *administer* has the word *minister* in it. To minister means to serve, and Paul lists administration as a spiritual gift (1 Cor. 12:28). Administrative principles can be found in the Bible, in both Old and New Testaments. And the application of those principles can help solve some common problems.

Poor Planning

Planning means setting the course for action and includes elements such as objectives, programming, scheduling, and budgeting.

Without effective objectives, churches cannot focus on the most important ministries and have little basis for evaluating results. What programs should they use? When can they be scheduled? How much will they cost? If they can't answer these questions, people get discouraged and do not want to be part of the ministry.

Years ago W. A. Criswell, former pastor of the First Baptist Church of Dallas, said to a group of pastors that his church could not do everything. At that time they had over twenty thousand members with multiple facilities and high-rise buildings for Sunday school. They conducted Christian schools, which included elementary through graduate study. They operated missions and ministries all over the area and around the world. They had a huge budget with a large staff. How could one church do more? Yet, Dr. Criswell repeatedly emphasized that they had to plan their priorities according to their resources, particularly personnel and finances.

Good planning motivates people to serve, because the priorities are set and they can see the direction the church is moving. Without good planning it will be difficult to get people excited and involved in ministry, or soon they will leave in frustration.

Poor Organization

Organization includes structure, delegation, and staff relationships. This function makes it possible for people to serve effectively.

Good structure helps people see how they fit into the overall ministry and how their roles relate to others. Problems arise when this is not clear. Individuals and groups go in different directions, and chaos replaces harmony.

The structure of a church grows out of its mission statement. Some churches may prefer loosely defined organization, others more carefully drawn organizational lines. Neither is necessarily wrong, but whatever is decided on will have greater effectiveness if all those involved understand the direction.

We might compare the structure of a church organization to a preplanned housing community. People know generally what to expect as they walk into each house for general overall room arrangement, but individual owners may freely express themselves with decorating and furniture layout. Structure does not destroy initiative or creativity; it sets general boundaries within which people may minister freely. Because the church is a living organism as well as an organization, her structure changes as her membership itself changes. The key is to keep this overall picture in front of the congregation so individual members do not wonder if the church community has a place for them.

Leaders who try to do everything themselves or who do not trust others with ministry responsibilities usually are poor delegators and weak in helping others use their gifts. Perhaps they feel that jobs will not be done adequately and the work of the church will be placed at risk.

Indeed, this may happen when tasks are not explained or supervised properly. People who do not delegate or who delegate poorly are usually limited to smaller church ministry opportunities they can personally control.

George Barna contributes to this discussion when he indicates that leaders of growing churches delegate responsibility without anxiety and use this as a way to empower other people to do ministry.[8]

One church noticed a severe turnover of workers in the Sunday school class for two-year-olds. Workers would volunteer for a few weeks and then quit. Some even left the church. On investigation leaders discovered that the ratio of children to workers went as high as 25:1. Early childhood specialists recommend a ratio of 3:1 or at the most 5:1 for this age group. No wonder people quit. The lack of adequate workers placed them in an impossible situation with no help or encouragement from the leadership. Recognizing the problem was caused by too few workers in the class, the leadership quickly recruited and trained a sufficient number of workers. This stopped the high turnover of workers, but even more important, greatly improved the quality of education in the class.

Of course, some leaders overdelegate and actually lose control of a situation. They give assignments but rarely check on progress. Leaders with this deficiency suffer from similar problems in developing effective ministry in those they supervise.

Poor organization causes people to wonder about the quality of the ministry and whether or not they want to be a part of it. They see symptoms of poor organization in last-minute teacher recruitment; in regular interruptions of classes to find emergency volunteers for children's classes; in poor communication to both workers and participants; in frequent class announcements promoting all kinds of ministry and offering requests; in disruption of teaching schedules on a regular basis; in lack of proper resources, and poor equipment and facilities; in placement of unprepared workers in positions of responsibility.

Someone with administrative gifts should work to keep the organization of the church in good condition. We are not suggesting more committees or complicated procedures and bottlenecks created by too many rules and regulations. On the contrary, proper organization will help the church carry on its mission with minimal interference and difficulty. If too many things keep getting in the way, we need to evaluate our ministry procedures. Potential workers will be demotivated by chaos; such an environment tends to keep people from volunteering or responding to an invitation to serve.

Poor Evaluation

Probably the weakest area of church ministry is evaluation. Perhaps we feel we should not evaluate the work of the Holy Spirit and hesitate to check up on the quality of ministry. But remember, the purpose of evaluation is improvement, not punishment. We ask questions on how well we are doing so that we can find even better ways to do the work.

Evaluation requires the setting of standards prior to implementing the work. Then we measure people's ministry according to the standards. From this evaluation we can determine ways to improve the work, helping us achieve the desired results. This will be expanded in chapter 7.

Recruitment Problems

Why do so many churches experience a shortage of workers? There is no simple answer to this question but we would like to offer several suggestions. Once a problem is well defined, work on the solution has begun.

Some Seem Indifferent to Their Responsibilities

Some church members apparently neglect or ignore God's call to serve. Marlene Wilson calls these nonworkers "pewsitters."[9] Perhaps some Christians get so involved in their ministries that they do not want help from others. They may gain a sense of power and authority by doing the work themselves. If this is the case, then the pewsitters do not sense the need to help.

This indifference certainly may be a spiritual problem, such as those discussed above. When people are not dedicated to the Lord's service, and when they put other things higher on their priority list, the work of the Lord does not look as attractive to them. Nothing short of a rededication to Christ and a change in priorities can correct this. Leaders should recognize this and help people discover God's purpose for their lives and regain a consistent relationship with the Lord.

Some Have Never Been Challenged to Become Involved in God's Work

People can be believers and church members, but many have not been approached to roll up their sleeves and accept the challenge of ministry. This may be difficult to believe if you are responsible to find volunteers. Perhaps you have invited everyone to serve, with announcements from the pulpit and articles in the church newsletter or bulletin. But this is not the way to enlist workers. *You can alert people to the general need for workers through public announcements, but you should enlist them through personal contact.*

When we consider something really important, we give it our personal attention. During a marriage seminar, the leader asked how many people had proposed to their wives with a letter duplicated on a copy machine. Obviously, no one had done so, but that is exactly how we often seek helpers in the church. One church was so desperate to find elders that they sent out eighty letters inviting people to volunteer for this most important position. How much better to discuss the position face to face.

Some Lack Confidence in Their Abilities

Past failures, what unthinking people have told them about themselves, the fear of failure, and the large responsibility before them could be several reasons people lack confidence to volunteer. Confidence can only be developed by being well prepared for the task at hand and enjoying the full support and encouragement of a leader. Preparation can come through training, observation, in-service training, practice teaching, coaching, and many other ways. More will be said about this in the section on training.

Some Misunderstand the Task

Church recruiters need to be specific in what they ask and expect from potential workers. They should help people understand that accepting a position does not entail a "life sentence." Potential volunteers see the awards given to teachers who have served for forty or fifty years and imagine they may be in line for a long tenure. They watch leaders place people in positions and never release them for other ministries. If leaders fail to provide further assistance for people to experience other opportunities of ministry, they may hamper their growth. Better to agree on a specific period of time, with the option to renew if agreeable to both parties.

Some Feel It Requires Much More Time and Effort Than They Can Contribute

Clear instructions with a job description will help solve this problem. Some positions do require greater amounts of time and effort, and these should be offered to people both qualified and able to perform the ministry. If people do not have the time necessary to fulfill a responsibility, help them select another ministry opportunity.

Some Have Been Improperly "Cataloged"

Church leaders often suffer from "hardening of the categories" when they look at potential workers. That is, they often think of people in only one place or conclude that certain people could never serve in any other significant way. They overlook them without doing a complete evaluation. Leaders need to break out of this procedure and look at people with a renewed optimism for service, to not overlook anyone, and to give everyone a chance to serve.

Some Are Too Busy

Statistics tell us that over 70 percent of the women in our country work outside the home. The traditional concept of the American family with a husband as the sole breadwinner, a wife who does not work outside the home, two children, a dog, and a cat represents less than 10 percent of the households. Yet it appears many churches continue to program for this arrangement. Add to this the increasing number of single-parent families, most headed by women, and you see that many in our population do not have the energy or time for heavy involvement in church ministry.

In the past the church has depended on women to carry on many of its ministries, especially in the area of education. With this resource limited, the volunteers are not readily available.

Just because people work outside the home, however, does not mean they cannot serve in some way. It does mean that their time commitment may be reduced because of these other responsibilities.

Some Must Cope with Dual-Career Households

A dual-career household poses special challenges to church leaders to help these busy families understand their need to minister and serve and the opportunities available to them. Some factors to consider:

1. Their opportunities for fellowship with other adult Christians may be severely limited. They may face the same problem finding good family time. A combination of service and fellowship activities is a possible solution. One family in this situation decided to do some occasional volunteer work at an inner-city congregation tied to their suburban church. As a family, they helped set up Christmas parties and deliver food baskets. Not only did they touch lives, but it gave special memories of time together to cherish.

2. Men and women with heavy career demands also often have talents badly needed by the church fellowship. Perhaps other members of the church family could take care of some household and maintenance tasks to free up otherwise occupied time. One gifted Bible study teacher found she could not carve out the necessary study time to prepare lessons when her work responsibilities expanded. Several women whom she had taught for years started cleaning her house

periodically, giving her adequate time for study—a beautiful example of body life.

3. As with all members of the Christian community, these time-pressed families need to understand that life is not divided into sacred and secular divisions. Work and worship intertwine in a healthy Christian life, for "whatever you do, whether in word or deed, do it all in the name of the Lord Jesus, giving thanks to God the Father through him" (Col. 3:17). Teach them to look for opportunities to spread the light of God's love at work. Friendship evangelism, lunchtime Bible studies, one-on-one listening sessions, high ethical standards, commitments to excellence—all have an effect on a dark world.

4. Because of this time problem, it will be necessary for a church to look at its ministries and try to break down some of the tasks into manageable units that can be assigned to different individuals. If it must settle for less time from more people, the task must be divided among faithful workers. Leaders need to assess ways more people will be able to contribute time and efforts to ministry.

One church that met in a school needed regular volunteers to set up the facilities for the services each week. Rather than make this a heavy weekly commitment for two people, they set up a schedule of three teams so that volunteers performed this task once every three weeks.

Some Make Different Choices in How They Use Their Free Time

Everyone, regardless of position or power, has the same 168 hours per week. The difference comes in how productive people make these hours and how they use them to serve the Lord through his church.

There are certain responsibilities that all people fulfill: to families, to work, to recreation, and to serve God. Some place too much time in one of these areas and live their lives out of balance. Many people, especially men, put so much effort into their work that they neglect their families. Others spend too much time on recreation, leaving little or no time for God and ministry.

People need to determine how to balance their lives and include each of these areas. Far too often, service to God is left off the list. Church leaders must challenge God's people to see this important aspect of their lives and accept the responsibility to serve God without neglecting other areas.

People are too busy and under too many pressures to continue to offer their free time to church activities that continually fail.[10] When there is no fulfilling reward, or when people are discouraged with ineffective ministry results, they will find other ways to spend their limited free time.

You may look at this list of problems and feel like throwing in the towel. Can you achieve significant ministry in the 1990s when you face so many reasons that keep people out of volunteer ministry? Yes! The work of the church will go forward, and you need to help more of the Lord's people find some place of effective ministry.

Application Activities

1. To what extent does the preaching and teaching ministry of your church proclaim the importance of personal involvement in ministry?

2. Do you present the importance of a personal involvement in church ministry to new church members in the orientation program?

3. To what extent does the prayer ministry of the church address this need?

4. In addition to prayer, does the church have a strategy in place to identify and recruit leaders?

5. Has your church clearly identified the priorities of ministry with biblical objectives?

6. Does your church fit the pattern of 10 percent of the people doing most of the work?

7. To what extent is communication effective in your church? How do you do it? How can it be improved?

8. To what extent do you evaluate ministries and individuals? What do you do to improve ministries and individuals?

9. Develop a list of your own reasons of why churches face a shortage of workers. Compare the list with the reasons suggested in this chapter. After each, write one or two possible ways to overcome it.

3

Steps to Effective Recruitment

Pam, a director of Christian education, saw a growing need for an additional worker in the room for two-year-olds during the first service. She had also for some time been observing David, a young teenager, who showed interest in working with young people. For several months he had been helping with the third and fourth grade class, but the class had an overload of helpers. The teacher there displayed a special talent for storytelling and attracted people just to listen to her tales.

Two weeks before recruitment for the next term was to begin, Pam asked David if he would go in with the two-year-olds for a couple of Sundays just to help out. He agreed a bit reluctantly, since he had no experience with that age group, but he was reassured that his responsibilities would be limited to playing with the children and helping with snacks and cleanup.

Pam made a point of checking frequently on David for the next two weeks. She noted with delight that he readily entered into the make-believe world of the two-year-old mind, obviously enjoying making truck sounds and eating pretend food. He even took the bathroom duty in stride.

After a quick consultation with his parents, Pam asked David if he would consider continuing with that responsibility for the next six months. David's eyes lit with delight at the prospect. He was having a wonderful time on Sunday mornings. He already knew each child's name and toy preferences. He soon matched parent to child and met a number of people new to the church, even introducing his parents to them.

Before David's term of service was over, a parental decision made it necessary for them to leave this church. David's first response on hearing the news was a tearful, "But Mom, what about the two-year-olds? They love me very much and will miss me if I have to leave." David had been an unlikely candidate for ministry before the church gave him an opportunity. But steps to effective recruitment begin with awareness of people and positions.

Looking for effective volunteers requires two areas of understanding: the ministry needs in the church and the people who are available to fill those needs. To recruit before understanding these two areas is like going to the grocery store without a shopping list. You will spend a lot of time looking and probably go home forgetting something you really needed.

A Ministry Inventory

The first step in recruiting volunteer workers is to discover the personnel and the needs of the church. Every church agency or group should participate by identifying their ministry requirements, including those not presently filled. Sometimes it is helpful to provide a chart or form for each ministry group. ⌡

Here is a sample chart for the Sunday school program.

Sunday School Staff

Title	Name of Person Serving
General Superintendent/Director	_____
Secretary	_____
Early Childhood Division	
coordinator	_____
cradle nursery director	_____
secretary	_____
teachers	_____
helpers	_____
nursery director	_____
secretary	_____
teachers	_____
helpers	_____
kindergarten director	_____
secretary	_____
teachers	_____
helpers	_____
Children's Division	
coordinator	_____
primary director	_____
secretary	_____
primary teachers	_____
primary-junior director	_____
secretary	_____
primary-junior teachers	_____
junior director	_____
secretary	_____
junior teachers	_____

Youth Division
    coordinator   _____
    secretary   _____
    junior high director   _____
    secretary   _____
    junior high teachers   _____
    high school director   _____
    secretary   _____
    high school teachers   _____

Adult Division
    coordinator   _____
    secretary   _____
    adult teachers   _____
    adult class leader   _____
    adult class officers   _____

As you customize this list to fit your church, you may add or subtract positions as necessary. Each agency of the church should come up with a similar listing of ministry positions. Write in the names of individuals serving in various positions and indicate all needs for additional workers by leaving spaces blank. From this church leaders can see how many volunteers presently serve and can discover current personnel needs.

This inventory forms a significant part of the strategy for recruiting volunteers. When people find themselves in financial difficulty, a good planner will first ask for a listing of assets and liabilities, basic information essential to chart a plan that can bring people to financial freedom. It works the same in church ministry. We must know our assets. Who presently serves and at what effectiveness? What areas are in need of new workers? What workers need additional training and encouragement?

As you write your staff inventory, look ahead to future ministries. Interestingly, planning ahead for future workers can make your present ministry more effective. It helps put current ministries in long-range perspective.

Some time ago, two fire engines drove into the seminary parking lot. Since they did not use sirens, there seemed to be no emergency. The fire department had come to the school to develop a plan of attack in case of a fire. They identified the electric and gas switches and then took the ladder truck around the back of the apartments to see if it would fit in the event of a necessary rescue. They checked every part of the campus, and when they finished, they had a written plan. They also presented several recommendations for fire prevention. Apparently, most fire departments spend the majority of their time in this type of activity rather than in fighting fires.

Such a good example for the church! Instead of merely "putting out fires" and then having to face the destructive aftermath, plan a strategy for "fire prevention." We need to devote more time to planning, training, and supervising workers, but this cannot be carried out if we constantly struggle to find the necessary workers.

The inventory mentioned above offers a good first step to "fire prevention" in church recruiting. It provides information necessary to complete the other steps in the process.

A Ministry Survey

The next step is to develop a survey of the entire congregation to discover potential volunteers. You develop the survey from the inventory suggested above and include every possible opportunity of ministry. On the survey provide a way for workers to indicate where they presently serve, have served in the past, feel equipped to serve, or are willing to serve in the future.

Designing the Survey

The survey below uses the words *active* (presently serving), *experienced* (have served in the past), *trained* (equipped to serve), and *interested* (possibly willing to serve). Notice that it asks for more information than volunteer service: important data for churches to know about their constituents.

Church Ministry Survey[1]

Mr. ____ Name _____ Sex ☐ M ☐ F

Ms. ____ Address _____

Miss ____ City _____ State____ Zip_____

Mrs. ____ Home phone_____ Business phone_____

Unlisted?_____

Second address _____

City_____ State _____ Zip_____

Dates at 2nd address____/____/____ to ____/____/____

Phone at 2nd address _____

Occupation _____ Employer_____

Birthday ____/____/____ Wedding anniversary ____/____/____

Marital status:

☐ single   ☐ married

☐ engaged   ☐ divorced

☐ widowed   ☐ separated

Children(s) Name(s) (Living at home):

_____	☐ M	☐ F
_____	☐ M	☐ F
_____	☐ M	☐ F
_____	☐ M	☐ F
_____	☐ M	☐ F

Relatives/Others living at same address:

_____ Doctor's phone _____

_____ Emergency contact _____

_____ Emergency phone_____

Relationship to church:

☐ Sunday school only   ☐ church member

☐ wife of member   ☐ husband of member

☐ nonmember   ☐ child of member

Sunday school dept._____ class_____

Occupational status:

☐ employed   ☐ self employed

☐ unemployed   ☐ student

☐ retired

No mail   ☐

No directory listing   ☐

No stewardship statement ☐

VOLUNTEERS FOR TODAY'S CHURCH

Groups/Skills/Interests:
1=Active 2=Experienced 3=Trained 4=Interested

Groups
___sanctuary choir
___children's choir
___youth choir
___Bible study
___men's fellowship
___women's fellowship
___youth clubs
___children's clubs
___
___

Admin/Office
___elder
___trustee
___deacon
___finance committee
___property committee
___nominating
___secretary
___typist
___bookkeeper
___writer/editor

Worship
___usher/greeter
___sound tech
___music committee
___worship committee
___decorations
___
___
___
___

Education
___Bible study leader
___teach preschool
___teach children
___teach youth
___teach adults
___Christian educ. com.
___
___
___

Outreach/Missions
___missions committee
___visitation
___membership committee
___evangelism explosion
___
___
___
___
___
___

Fellowship
___kitchen committee
___social committee
___
___
___
___
___
___

Community Services
___foster home
___helping elderly
___hospital volunteer
___youth work
___
___
___
___

Spiritual Gifts
___administration
___exhortation
___giving
___mercy
___prophecy
___serving/helping
___teaching
___
___

Promotion
___advertising
___poster art
___public relations
___public speaking
___publicity/edit
___sign painting
___tv/radio
___writing
___
___
___

Stewardship
___estate planning
___investments
___foundations
___
___
___
___
___
___

Technical
___media
___computer
___lighting
___mechanic
___printer
___sound/lighting
___video
___chauffeur license
___pick up
___

Repair/Construction
___carpenter
___carpet layer
___electrician
___gardener
___handyman
___glazier
___janitor
___landscaper
___mason
___painter
___plumber

Vocal Music
___soprano
___alto
___tenor
___bass
___soloist
___small group
___

Instrumental Music
___piano
___organ
___strings
___woodwind
___brass
___percussion
___guitar
___

Child Care
___church nursery
___in homes
___in own home
___days
___evenings
___weekends
___

Kitchen
___cleanup
___decorations
___receptions
___
___
___

Drama
___acting
___choreography
___directing
___makeup
___set construction
___set design
___stage crew
___

When each church group lists its ministry opportunities on the form, it becomes a complete list of needed personnel. Be sure to include all groups such as music, men's and women's ministry, Bible studies, discipleship groups, community ministries, weekday ministries, office work, maintenance, repair, painting, electrical—everything. This important group project communicates to the congregation the many opportunities of church ministry. Adjust the survey to fit your church.

Administering the Survey

When you administer the survey, you want the largest possible participation. Here, then, is a suggested approach.

1. Ask the pastor to preach a series of sermons on the importance of serving the Lord in the church and the personal fulfillment such a ministry brings.

2. Use newsletters, bulletins, bulletin boards, and posters to emphasize the theme of serving the church.

3. Mail a letter, including a copy of the survey, to every member of the congregation asking that the form be returned to the church. Just prior to "Survey Sunday," send a postcard to remind people to bring their completed surveys. Perhaps you could have the surveys completed in adult classes and take a few minutes in the worship service for those who were not in the classes. A third possibility is to take the survey during the worship service. Do what works best for you; find a way to have the largest number of people participate.

4. At a special Sunday morning service, ask the people to bring their completed surveys to the front and

offer a prayer of dedication. Be sure to have extra surveys available.

Following "Survey Sunday," announce that those who did not turn in their surveys should bring them to the church by a set deadline. Follow up those still missing without "hounding" anyone.

Many churches go this far but fail to take full advantage of the opportunity. Yes, you might discover some new workers just by looking over the forms, but you want more lasting results. Marlene Wilson makes this perceptive comment about the use, or misuse, of surveys: *"Time and talent sheets have helped officially reject people's gifts every year. These surveys should never be filled out if they are not going to be used. It tells people who are never called on either that their gifts are not needed or that they are of little value. Many pewsitters have received that message very clearly."*[2]

Collate the data, creating a file for each position and one for each individual. Write a card or letter of appreciation to everyone who completed a survey. Acknowledge what they volunteered to do and indicate when you will contact them for an interview. Inform them about training opportunities. If there are no openings at present in areas of their interest, indicate that, too, and tell them that they will be contacted as soon as some ministry is available.

One church used a computerized ministry survey form much like the one above. They asked people to volunteer for positions of ministry. One gentleman admitted that he had volunteered for several ministry opportunities and waited for the church leaders to contact him. Four years passed, and he never heard a word. The failure to communicate with the man cannot be blamed on computer error. The leadership simply did not use the results of the survey. If people make the effort to complete the survey, leaders need to make the effort to thank them and follow up their responses.

Utilizing the Results

Who manages the list of volunteers? How can each ministry in the church have equal access to the names? Many churches appoint a person to supervise volunteer recruitment who works with a special committee to manage the process. The task carries a major responsibility and requires much time. It also has potential to involve more and more people, which results in a more effective church ministry.

The information must be kept current. Organize these data so they can be retrieved easily. Are some folks overloaded with too many tasks, while others merely watch? Adequate and accurate information will help leaders make decisions about present and future ministries and whether or not they can be staffed with volunteers.

At each new-member orientation use the surveys along with a good introduction to all the church's ministries. This strategy will help the church keep the survey information up-to-date and eliminate the need to take a survey each year.

Finding New Volunteers

All church leaders should be on the lookout for potential workers. Adult Sunday school teachers can identify people in their classes who are ready to serve as teachers or workers in other ministries. Sometimes teachers are reluctant to identify potential leaders because they do not want them to leave their classes.

A proper theology of ministry will counter this objection and help all teachers discover that those who have benefited from their teaching now need to serve others. That's discipleship.

Observation

Being on the lookout requires a great deal of discernment. We want to avoid the warm-body syndrome—the idea that anyone will do for a volunteer position as long as he or she is alive and breathing. *Keep uppermost in mind the purpose of church leadership: to equip believers for the work of the ministry, not just to make sure that "churchy" jobs get done.* Wilson makes four suggestions to help keep the proper perspective:

1. "Slots" must become ministries;
2. "Members" must become unique individuals;
3. "Oughts and shoulds" must become "may I's" of love;
4. "Turns" must become opportunities to share gifts.[3]

Believers come to maturity in Christ as they learn to serve in the church; therefore, leaders have a responsibility to help identify the uniqueness that each individual brings to the ministry. Vern Heidebrecht puts it well:

Most seminary students go through a discernment process to enable them in entering ministries for which they are best suited. Usually this special discernment time includes calling several seminary professors, family members, fellow students, and a pastoral mentor for insights and counsel. This is a sensitive, yet confrontational exercise which is essential for the seminarian to have discernment as to his or her ministry. After all, the entire seminary experience is designed to place individuals into effective ministry.

What is good for the seminarian is also good for the lay person. Our theology clearly teaches us that all Christians are called to ministry, yet we really do struggle with knowing what this means in practical terms. If it is true that Jesus was addressing all believers when he announced, "You did not choose me, but I chose you and appointed you to go and bear fruit, fruit that would last" (John 15:16), then we have an agenda to work on for all the church members.

Ask yourself: "How is the call of Christ affirmed for the laity? Where and how are we taking seriously the equipping ministry for them? And are we helping each person in a serious way to develop a significant ministry?" These are questions that need to come center stage onto our agenda as a church. To miss this critical issue is to overlook the nature of the church and its calling.[4]

Ministry Fair

A ministry fair provides more than exposure to ministry opportunities; it is also an effective way for the congregation to see how the church budget is used to support these ministries. Rather than just reading a line item on the budget page, people can talk with those serving in the ministries and see how resources are used.

Ask every ministry of the church to prepare a display to communicate to the congregation what that ministry is all about, how it fits into the mission statement of the church, and what are its current needs. Arrange the displays in a prominent location, like the narthex, so those attending worship services will have opportunity to visit the displays.

Each display should have handouts that include the church budget, the focus of the ministry, the current needs, and how interested people in the congregation can assist. Refreshments in the area facilitate an informal atmosphere for meaningful discussions.

Boys' and girls' clubs program workers can wear their uniforms; Sunday school leaders can display the curriculum as well as group projects; the missions committee can have a world map showing where the church-supported missionaries serve, as well as prayer lists and missionary opportunities; youth ministries can show slides of mission trips or retreats; and local mission groups supported by the church can have a display.

The ministry fair may not be the best time to recruit workers for ministries, but it does educate the congregation on the many possibilities available. Of course, leaders will further engage people who express an interest.

Public Announcements

Be careful to make ministry opportunities announcements general in nature. If you make them specific (like asking for a first-grade Sunday school teacher) you may attract someone unqualified for the position. Announce the needs that exist in various areas and provide an easy way for people who may be interested to respond.

In giving announcements in the worship service about volunteer needs, try to be creative. One pastor explained how important he felt the children's Sunday school ministry of the church was and said, "If teaching our children the Word of God were the only ministry we had, it would be worth our existence as a church!"

He then called one of the children's leaders to the platform for a brief interview and asked three questions. What preparation is needed to teach in the children's ministry? She replied, "A love for the Lord and a love for children." Why don't people volunteer to teach? "Perhaps they feel inadequate and don't see the need." How can interested people find out about helping in the children's department? She gave names to contact, suggested a visit to the special display in the narthex where workers were ready to answer questions and provide information, and directed people to call the church office or indicate interest on the church registration card.

Notice that the pastor needs to show his complete support for the ministry. This not only encourages the present workers but also prompts people to volunteer.

In a large church the staff cannot know all the people and the availability of potential workers. It becomes important for everyone to help with recruitment. When done properly, it is everyone's job.

Recruiting Volunteers

We have all heard stories of people pressed into service at the last minute, and who, over the years, earned awards for faithfulness. Sure, sometimes these last-minute emergency appeals work but there is a much better way. Instead, follow David Rambo's suggestions as you approach people for service:

> Look over your congregation in a totally new light. What are the possibilities of each one? What would it be like if all of them exercised their spiritual gifts?

Make it your goal to discover those gifts, and then put them to work.

Dream dreams for them. Most of our people have no idea of what they are capable of, but they long to do what is significant, something that includes their local church and reaches beyond to the large world of need.

Develop them into leaders and servants. Luther's Reformation is still incomplete. Every believer is a priest in the sense that he or she has an important part in the ministry of the church. The pastor needs to guide this development.

Give them meaningful ministries. Leith Anderson in *Dying for Change* notes that 96 percent of energy and time in work by the laity goes toward maintenance of the status quo. For effective outreach in the community, motivate and prepare the best of your lay people.[5]

Several years ago, after serving on a church staff for nearly fourteen years, Dennis resigned because of a physical problem. The family then joined a different church, not as staff but as regular members. After a few weeks the director of the young-adult department approached Dennis about teaching in this department. She asked if she could come by the house to discuss the position.

She arrived on time and talked about all the important issues: the spiritual requirements of teachers, the curricular materials to be used, the regular teachers' meeting (which also provided training), the importance of outside contact with members and prospects through visitation and social activities, and some needs of the people in the class. She indicated that the appointment would be one year and completed the interview by leading in prayer, asking the Lord to direct in any decision about the class. Then she said she would check back in a week.

This was no last-minute request. Dennis sensed no desperation on the part of the recruiter. He was not the only person on earth who could teach the class. The church would not shut down if he refused. This experience assured him that the church leaders responsibly managed their ministry. It challenged him to accept the position.

Look again at the elements included in this effective interview.

1. The recruiter highlighted the significance of the position by making an appointment to discuss the opportunity. No last-minute cries for help.

2. Using the Scripture, she underscored the importance of teaching the Word of God. This was not just another job but a position of significance.

3. Dennis heard that teachers should be spiritually mature and knowledgeable about God's Word. Qualification includes both.

4. He understood that teachers in this department do not just do "their own thing" but teach according to the curriculum plan of the church.

5. The church expected attendance at teachers' meetings for planning, training, prayer, and also for preparation.

6. The recruiter emphasized that teaching also requires outside contact with class members and prospects. Teaching is more than what happens on Sunday morning.

7. The position covered one year, not a "life sentence." Of course, the assignment could be renewed after one year if agreeable to both parties.

8. Finally, the recruiter gave adequate time to make the decision before she returned.

Sometimes, when desperate to find workers, church recruiters accept anyone willing. This usually backfires and eventually causes many additional problems. In fact, many of the problems with ineffective workers result from a poor recruitment experience. If people are not told what is expected of them, the system has no right to enforce requirements. But if everything is carefully explained, and they accept a position, they are responsible to fulfill their commitments. Remember, people rarely perform above the level at which they are recruited.

To review, first, identify ministry opportunities from the inventory. Then, develop and administer the survey to find possible workers for a ministry. These workers must be properly recruited and will require training and supervision. These topics are further addressed in later chapters.

Application Activities

1. Does your church spend most of its time meeting immediate recruitment needs or planning for future needs? What is the proper balance between the two? What can you do to move a church from the crisis approach to that of future planning?

2. Does your church have a written list of every possible ministry position? How could such a list be developed? Who should lead the process?

3. Does the church have an up-to-date ministry survey of the congregation? Do you use it effectively? If you do not have this important information available, use the suggestions in this chapter to develop and administer a survey in your church. Set up a time

frame in which to identify individuals or groups responsible.

4. Why is it important to continue to contact people after you have presented a ministry opportunity for which they volunteered on a survey? What are some practical ways this can be done?

5. How can your church recruit people for the many positions identified in the inventory? Who will take responsibility for this task? Do you need to assign a special committee or is there such a group presently serving? How can your church get such a group functioning?

6. Discuss your reaction to the list of essential elements in the recruitment interview. Do you consider them realistic for your situation? What would you change? What would you keep?

7. Why was it stated that most problems in working with volunteers can be traced to the recruitment interview?

4

Stopping Attrition
of Volunteers

For several years Karen attended the business and professional women's Bible study at her church. Eventually she began to serve as a leader for the small-group discussion times. Because she taught first grade during the day, she gave her one evening a week with adult women priority as a time of refreshment and rebuilding. When the Bible study leader asked Karen to take over administration of the entire program, she readily agreed to do so.

Karen's talents blossomed as she discovered new ways to express her immense creativity. She instituted an ambitious program to encourage the women to memorize large portions of Scripture, melting down initial resistance with her enthusiasm and encouragement. Attendance increased, with the initial core of women feeling comfortable enough to invite their co-workers and neighbors. Karen recruited more group leaders and learned to delegate administrative tasks to them.

The one area in which Karen did not wish to assume responsibility was the actual Bible teaching. The regular instructor understood this and did not press her. During one year, however, the instructor faced some family emergencies, which necessitated many periodic absences from her post. Karen, with great fear, had to fill in at the last minute. After stumbling a few times, she discovered that her individual style of teaching, although quite different from the regular instructor's, still ministered to the women. After that particularly difficult year she told the instructor, "I think I learned more when you weren't here than when you were! As much as I appreciate your teaching, it was very important for me to learn that I could teach, too. I also had to learn that I couldn't teach like you do, and it's fine for me to be different."

Then Karen had her long-awaited first child. She decided to take a break from teaching first grade for several years. She now had the freedom to attend the daytime Bible study composed mostly of mothers with young children. Although her talents could certainly be used there, her presence had been essential to the evening group. The evening Bible study teacher found herself overloaded with family responsibilities that mandated a year off. Furthermore, one of the key group leaders, an older woman with immense warmth and wisdom, greatly loved by the women in the group, had to leave the church. Within a short time, an active, thriving ministry had shrunk to less than a third of its former size, its very existence in question.

When churches work so hard to enlist, train, and place volunteers into service opportunities in the church, they should do all they can to keep them on the job. Volunteer turnover in some churches may be as high as 25 percent a year. For a church with a volunteer staff of one hundred, this means that twenty-five new volunteers must be found each year to replace those retiring, resigning, or taking different positions. A new volunteer must be found nearly every other week just to keep up with the present requirements in such a congregation, and that does not account for growth or possible new ministries.

Why is retention of volunteers a problem? Why do people quit even after they have found satisfaction in a volunteer position? What causes this change of heart? Have they lost interest in serving the Lord in the church? Have their circumstances changed? Do they have problems with their ministry positions and feel the only way out is to quit?

Perhaps all these questions help focus on the reasons why retention of volunteers poses a problem. Attrition of volunteers complicates the recruitment task and in many cases seriously affects the work of the church. It takes time to know and trust people. If volunteers and leaders of the various ministries are replaced too often, a sense of frustration and concern arises.

Let's look at some of the reasons for attrition and several suggestions about what can be done to reverse this serious trend.

7 - follow list

Lack of Appreciation

Have you ever worked for a supervisor who never let you know how well you were doing, who appreciated his employees, but it was not his style to say so? Perhaps he was like the man who never told his wife he loved her. When questioned, he responded that he told her he loved her the day they were married, and if anything changed, he would be sure to let her know. Not many of us want that kind of relationship.

Compliments and Encouragement

Here is a basic principle of ministry all leaders must understand: The success of leaders depends on the success of those working with them. *Success* is a positive word to indicate that leaders can accomplish what God truly intends for them in an effective and faithful way. Leaders sincerely want those serving with them to be successful so that the work of the Lord and the church will go forward. That's how biblical leadership works. It requires much more than merely showing appreciation, but without it, people will not serve as they could.

One time, while leading a workshop at a Sunday school convention, Dennis emphasized the importance of showing appreciation. One man asked if by showing appreciation we deny folks a future reward from God. Dennis stood stunned, wondering what kind of Bible interpretation could bring one to such a conclusion. Yes, the Scriptures do indicate that Christians will receive rewards according to their labor, but that hardly relieves their responsibility to affirm brothers and sisters in present life. Appreciation offers just one way to help people be fulfilled in their ministry positions.

Availability

Leaders show appreciation to people by being available when they serve. Too many people enlisted to serve are placed in a position and left on their own for weeks, even months, at a time.

One church had a difficult time keeping volunteers in the early childhood department. It seemed that each week there were several last-minute "emergency" calls for volunteers. Somebody discovered that the workers felt left alone, thinking that the leaders did not know or care about what they were doing. In this large church the pastor preached at two worship services, making it difficult for him to visit this department and encourage the workers. He did care about the volunteers, and their assumption was entirely wrong, but lack of contact led them to feel isolated and unimportant.

Perhaps the pastor could visit a planning meeting and show his appreciation. Even if he had to come into the worship service late once in a while, it would be good to stop by the department and show how much he valued its ministry. Leaders need to be present where people serve and look for opportunities to give words of affirmation. One of the most important leadership challenges is to help people understand that their work really makes a difference.

Visibility

You cannot carry out effective supervision from behind a desk. Pastors, ministers of Christian education, Sunday school superintendents, ministry coordinators, and members of the Christian education committee all need to be visible.

Ministry supervisors should personally greet every worker in his or her area of responsibility each Sunday. We need to show how much we really care. Be alert and sensitive to possible needs and do what you can to meet them. Offer suggestions when requested and remind your colleagues of forthcoming events such as training opportunities and special church activities.

Weekly one-on-one contact affords a wonderful way to show appreciation, and it is a powerful mode of communication.

Regular Meetings

Supervision also involves meeting with volunteers on a regular basis. Sit down together, pray together, share dreams together, and work to make the ministry the best it possibly can be. Encourage volunteers and suggest how they can improve their ministry. Use these times as equipping and training opportunities. More on this in chapter 6.

Application

You can show appreciation by writing notes and cards throughout the year. The end of the year is a special time when people have performed a task especially well or when a class has received special recognition. Some leaders even keep a list of birthdays and special events and send cards regularly.

Use announcements and notes in the Sunday bulletin, the church newsletter, and other publications to show that you consider every ministry important. Every effort is most beneficial.

Some churches plan an annual appreciation banquet served by the board or staff members or, perhaps, by people who have benefited from the ministries of those being recognized. Make sure the guests of honor are not asked to work in any way at the banquet.

People do not serve in churches for monetary gain, but churches can certainly give some kind of gift or award to those who have faithfully served during the year. Consider a gift certificate from a Christian bookstore, or scholarship assistance to area training events such as Sunday school conventions, community Bible school programs, and seminars.

However you do it, show appreciation to workers and keep people excited with their ministry. Public affirmation provides genuine motivation. More important, it's biblical.

Misplacement in Ministry Positions

Notice how intricately and brilliantly the human body is designed. Nothing can do a hand's job nearly as well as a hand can. Those who lose the use of their hands often find other body parts, especially the foot, can replace some of the functions of the hand but not with the same efficiency. *Star Trek* fans may have noticed an interesting fact. As creative as their writers and designers are, the vast majority of beings that the *Enterprise* crew encounters have the same general build as the Creator-designed human body. It works very well.

According to the Scriptures, God planned for the church body to function like the human body, with the hand doing a hand's work and an eye doing an eye's work (Rom. 12; 1 Cor. 12). Unfortunately, it is not often easy to discern elbows from wrist joints when working with complex and sin-scarred human beings. Marlene Wilson expresses her amazement at the many different ways individuals define personal challenges or achievement.

Here is an exercise I have used extensively in groups to illustrate this fact. Have all participants think of the one job they have had (volunteer or paid) that they liked the best and the one they like the least. As people share their answers, they are surprised to discover that almost everyone's favorite job is someone else's least favorite, and that there is someone who enjoys almost any job (even fund raising, teaching teenagers, book-keeping, cooking, filing, and long-range planning).

This exercise also is helpful in freeing leaders to be more effective and creative delegators. People can understand why they are reluctant to delegate what they themselves enjoy doing. But they fail to realize how often they hesitate delegating what they dislike doing because they feel guilty about "dumping" it on someone else. What they begin to realize through this exercise is that the tasks they dislike may very well be someone else's favorite thing to do. If they would only become more inventive in sharing their work and in finding ways to invite more people to partici-pate, they would see that there is a right person for every job.[1]

This is interesting and a good idea for group discussion with your volunteers.

We have already explained the helpfulness of the ministry survey. As you look over your ministry needs, you might consider categorizing them into types of jobs. General categories can include the following:

1. Maintenance activities: those that involve the physical appearance of the building and grounds.
2. Clerical support: these days will probably require some computer or word-processor knowledge.
3. Personal contact responsibilities: a wide category encompassing those who assume visitation, counseling, and teaching ministries.
4. Performance tasks: for those who have had train-ing in music, drama, leading worship, etc.
5. Planning activities: the type of committee work that sees to it that the church runs smoothly.[2]

After you define ministry categories, think about the people whom God has entrusted to you to equip. Talk with them, help them see and articulate their goals, their hopes, their dreams. Be careful not to box them in, nor to assume that just because they do a task for regular employment their volunteer work should follow the same patterns. Douglas Johnson writes:

> This common assumption that persons who make their livelihood in certain professions are willing to use their expertise in a volunteer manner for the church is not supported by fact in many instances. Several persons accept occupation-oriented, volunteer work because they feel they should. Others do not do any volunteer work because they are not willing to be limited by their profession. Persons are in occupations due to early life choices. During the intervening years, interests have developed and hobbies have expanded that are more fulfilling than the occupation. The person has grown in ways other than their life's work. These ways are keys to happiness and fulfillment for the person now.[3]

When we place volunteers in areas for which God has gifted and equipped them, we minimize the probability of burnout, disenchantment with the church, and disappointment with the ministry.[4]

When we discover people improperly placed, we must go to them and admit the problem. Using the ministry survey, look for a place of service in which they can serve effectively according to their gifts and calling. Make the transition as smooth as possible, but do not ignore the problem; it will only get worse.

Carl George offers some very practical suggestions for recognizing, enlisting, and affirming workers in the church, suggestions closely related to the issue of spiritual gifts.

1. Study the subject of spiritual gifts in depth.
2. Learn to recognize people's gifts from their criticisms and suggestions.
3. Make it a practice to affirm the gifts you see.
4. Ask for help in the church according to gifts discerned.[5]

Personality Clashes

Sometimes human relations problems seem more difficult when in churches and Christian organizations. Some folks say Christians should let the grace of God work out these problems and not try to deal with them on their own. Certainly church leaders do not have time to deal with every personality problem among their workers, but wisdom precludes placing workers together who do not get along very well. The team approach to ministry is crucial, for personality conflicts may prohibit the possibility of good teamwork.

Try to match people who can work together effectively. When problems arise, they should be dealt with immediately by using biblical guidelines. Do not allow volunteer staff problems to continue week after week or you will be in danger of destroying morale and negatively affecting the people whom the volunteers serve.

Meeting together on a regular basis, sharing and praying about each other's needs and concerns, and sensing a common vision for the ministry can help minimize personality clashes among volunteers.

Often it appears that people not directly involved in a ministry seem most vocal in their complaints and feelings about others. There is a principle here: The more we involve people in significant ministry and the more they sense the urgency of that ministry, the fewer personality clashes come up to destroy valuable ministry time.

They say that in military combat, those behind the major lines of battle do most of the complaining, while those up front focus their efforts on working together to win the battle. In fact, their very survival depends on teamwork.

Inadequate Facilities and Equipment

Though lack of resources is not the major reason for attrition of volunteers, it does contribute to the problem. People do not need the finest, most expensive classrooms in which to teach the Word of God, but neither do they want a shoddy, dirty, poorly equipped facility.

A church communicates how it feels about a certain ministry by the way it provides for that ministry. Volunteers understand this quite well. Of course, sometimes a church cannot afford to do better, but it can make certain that rooms are clean and in the best possible condition. Perhaps it cannot afford to purchase all the possible curricular materials, but it can and should supply some.

Careful planning should correct many of these problems. Survey the needs and make a list of everything that should be done with regard to facilities, equipment, and resources. Set up a schedule to purchase and distribute necessary items. Some things can be done immediately, like cleaning up a room. Others will take longer, like painting, securing adequate chairs, ordering curriculum materials, or purchasing overhead projectors and screens. Such items should be included in a budget with a definite schedule. People tend to be more patient if they know that the church wants to correct the problems. Too many disappointments will lead to eventual resignations, so keep these important issues before the church leaders.

Inadequate Training

People lose interest in ministries that they do not know how to perform. An entire chapter of this book addresses this critical need of training, but we mention it here as well.

Sometimes seminary students are assigned to interview a Sunday school superintendent or the teacher responsible for securing volunteers in that church's educational ministry. After asking how people are found and recruited, the student asks about training. Often at this point the interviewee gets nervous and uncomfortable. The common response is that there has not been time to schedule a training time or perhaps that the curriculum materials are easy to use and self-explanatory. Of course, some churches do provide training for their volunteers on a regular basis.

Without training, the attrition rate will rise, because people are not prepared for the tasks they face. Training offers a basic way to keep volunteers on the job, and that training should take place both before they begin the ministry and while they are in the process. See chapter 6 for additional information on equipping and training.

Lost Peer Fellowship

This problem usually occurs with volunteers in the early childhood and children's departments, though it can be found with youth volunteers and even those who serve adults.

As social beings, all of us need relationships with others. Remember the important element of fellowship found in the mission statement suggested in chapter 1. The church needs to provide fellowship opportunities, not only because that is scriptural but because we need human contact to be fulfilled in our lives.

This problem appears when volunteers spend all their time with a selected age group and lose contact with those their own age. A youth director discovered this when a group of church leaders came to his home for a surprise birthday party. Conversation was difficult, because the group did not act like teenagers. He tried to liven up the group with games and activities, but they did not respond. He finally realized what had happened. He had lost the ability to relate to his peers because he spent so much time with young people.

Often people leave an adult Sunday school class to teach children or youth. But that adult class or fellowship group can keep them as "associate" members and invite them to participate in the activities of the class, though they might not attend the teaching time on Sunday morning.

If people teach every Sunday, they need a class or group during the week in which they can participate as learners, too. This will provide another opportunity for that important adult contact.

If people miss the worship service (usually because of a children's church program) they will need to be informed of announcements and activities that make it possible to have these important fellowship contacts. If you tape worship services (or at least the message), why not give free copies to all volunteers unable to attend.

Providing this balance for volunteers is essential so they can be fulfilled in both their ministries and their need for fellowship.

Think again of Karen at the beginning of the chapter. What might have kept her in that important leadership position and enabled the women's ministry to continue effectively? Even if the regular instructor did show appreciation and there was no evidence of a serious personality clash, the strong possibility exists that effective training and peer fellowship were both missing ingredients. We cannot afford to be out finding new Karens every month or even every year. Careful attention to the six problems identified in this chapter will go a long way toward stopping the attrition of volunteers in your church.

Application Activities

1. Analyze the percentage of volunteer turnover your church experiences in a year. Is it higher or lower than the normal 25 percent?

2. With a group of leaders, brainstorm the reasons for turnover of volunteers in your church. Compare the reasons you list with those presented in this chapter. In what areas are you doing a good job and in what areas do you need improvement?

3. Look carefully at reasons given for the turnover of volunteers in your church. For those over which you have some control, offer several specific suggestions on how to correct the problems. (You really have no control over people moving from a community or serious illnesses which require resignations.) This critical exercise can help your church not only keep volunteers serving but keep them fulfilled in ministry.

4. To what extent does your church express appreciation to volunteers who serve faithfully week after week? Select some of the suggestions for appreciation in this chapter or add to the list and plan to implement some of them with your volunteers this year.

5. Are you aware of volunteers in your church who are not doing a good job in their ministry? Analyze the reason or reasons to determine if they need more training and supervision or if they may be serving in the wrong positions. Regardless of the cause, what steps will you take to empower the workers in making the ministry more effective and satisfying to them? Utilize the recommendations provided in this chapter.

6. What personality clashes do you see in your church? What can be done to resolve this common problem? Do people spend more time complaining than serving? What can you do to get volunteers focusing more on the ministry than on each other and their particular disagreements?

7. Complete a facilities, equipment, and resources inventory for your educational ministry. Make a list of needs and desires. Develop a priority listing, indicating which things can be done immediately and which things will need to be scheduled for future action. Set up a timetable, with workdays scheduled along with proper financing. At what point in time will you have this important area where you want it to be?

8. Analyze your educational ministry to see if people who serve are missing out on important fellowship opportunities with their peers. If this is a problem, use some of the suggestions provided in this chapter to try to make it possible for volunteers to be part of a social group as well as the group they are teaching.

5

Keeping Workers Fulfilled: Motivation

A re either Walt or Jill around? We can't get this program going without them." Walt and Jill, husband and wife and both electronics geniuses, had proved their worth to the church over and over again. Whenever someone needed audiovisual equipment to be set up, either Walt or Jill showed up to do it.

An interesting couple talented in the same area, both were equally shy. Both preferred at all times to stay behind the scenes and have no public or up front roles. One frequent teacher at the church commented, "It always gave me a feeling of reassurance to see them there when I was going to speak. I knew they would manage the sound equipment well, and the taping would be done as professionally as possible, given the limitations of their equipment. In my opinion, these two people will be given great honor in heaven for their faithful service."

But Walt and Jill no longer serve at that church. What happened? Jill's response: "Do you remember the year Walt became so ill, and the doctors couldn't seem to diagnose the problem? Even though we have been members of this congregation for a long time, it seemed like we were invisible to the pastoral staff. We needed some support, but we were ignored."

Walt, normally quiet about his feelings, added, "All new equipment is being installed in the meeting room the church just finished building. I'm not familiar with the way it works, but I'm sure I could learn it. But the assistant pastor told me they were going to find someone else to run it. Why didn't he give me a chance?"

In the last chapter were listed some of the reasons for the high attrition of ministry volunteers and suggestions on how to overcome some of these problems. This chapter focuses on three important ways to keep volunteers: through communication, team relationships, and motivation.

Keeping Communication Channels Open

Effective communication includes the sending and receiving of information to bring about understanding, agreement, acceptance, and/or a favorable response. Active listening forms an essential part.

Listening is enhanced by concentrating on what is being said. Acknowledge what you are hearing with brief verbal comments and ask questions. Periodically paraphrase to increase comprehension. Summarize when the person is finished to see if you misunderstood something that may need to be corrected.

Values of Communication

Communication facilitates good relationships with others, while poor communication inhibits them. Interaction with others in a group requires a climate in which individual ideas can be modified to become the best possible solutions to the group's problems.

This factor dominates every kind of relationship. Communication breakdown causes major personality clashes, serious disagreements, breakup of marriages, church splits, and the loss of important workers in the ministry.

Volunteers need to know what is happening in ministry areas they serve. Keeping basic information from workers destroys trust in the leaders and breeds unnecessary suspicion. The more people know about plans and projects, the more they are likely to give their best efforts.

Channels of Communication

Information flow improves when people who do the work help plan the work. When people know from the beginning what is happening, they have a chance to participate in decision making.

One small church had four Sunday school classes in the four corners of the auditorium and two more separated by a small partition in the balcony. The noise problem was compounded by the fact that one of the teachers spoke very softly and the teacher nearest him was quite loud. The obvious solution was to get one to speak up and the other to tone down, but this did not work.

When the six teachers met to discuss the problem, they decided to have the "soft teacher" move his class to the balcony. They felt the teacher currently in the balcony could hold his own with the other adult teacher. When the class members came on Sunday morning they all knew where to go, because their teachers had called them during the week about the change. The change worked, because those involved participated in planning the solution. Imagine what it would have been like if one person had made a decision to switch classes and then merely told students when they came to class. Both teachers and students would have been upset, and the attempt at problem-solving would have met major resistance.

How do the workers in your church learn about changes, especially those affecting them directly? If they must miss worship services because of ministry, how do they find out about the announcements? Workers who feel isolated lose interest and quickly become part of the attrition problem.

Problems in Communication

Good communication is difficult to achieve. Just because we announce something does not mean it was heard or understood. In fact, there is a high possibility many did not understand, and sometimes people think they hear announcements that were never made.

If we want to make certain a message gets across to people and that they receive it, we need to send it on at least five channels from among the following: public announcements, printed announcements in bulletins, phone calls, posters, bulletin boards, Sunday school class announcements, special mailings, personal contacts, and promotion in the church newsletter.

Announcements must be repeated, because people would rather talk than listen. In a worship service, for example, announce the hymn number only once and see how many did not catch it. When the President of the United States addresses the nation on television, newscasters tell us beforehand what he will say. Then he says it. After the speech the newscasters repeat it again. The newspaper the next morning prints a copy of the address, followed by a synopsis in news magazines the next week. Our society expects information to be repeated. If we want people to know about our ministries, we must do the same.

The best way to communicate is face to face. When we send letters or notes and print announcements in newsletters and bulletins, we have no way of knowing how effective this is because of lack of feedback. One-on-one communication can clarify misunderstanding as we ask questions about the message to see if people received it as sent *and* if they have accepted it. Obviously this takes a great deal more time, but in the end it will be more effective.

People working in ministry positions must not overlook the importance of meeting together on a regular basis. This meeting should include prayer, planning, preparation, training, and fellowship. Meet for a specific purpose and make it worthwhile for all who attend. Meeting just to meet wastes time, but well-planned meetings that include these elements will result in effective communication and a greater sense of loyalty to the ministry.

Someone has said that you cannot *overcommunicate*. Rather, the problem in churches is definitely *undercommunication*. When people active in ministry do not know what is going on they lose their motivation for service and do not feel a part of the team.

Building a Team Relationship

Return for a moment to Walt and Jill to see what killed their motivation. They were willing and eager to serve and for years did so faithfully and well. It was not necessary to challenge them, to push them into service in any way. It seemed adequate for them to know they were needed.

Strangely, their quiet and gentle spirits worked against them. When Walt's health problems hit, their small group of intimate friends did what they could to help, but could not carry the burden alone. Although a general appeal was made, few others responded. In the meantime, a person with a more visible ministry in the church also faced illness, and many offered help.

Walt and Jill had gained their skill in electronics from their educational and employment backgrounds. Neither had obtained a college degree. Because of their shyness and poorly developed communication skills, the church leaders did not perceive them as particularly capable of learning the intricacies of complicated new equipment. Leaders did not ask but merely assumed they were incapable.

Leaders' Roles

To the leaders Walt and Jill were "faithful worker bees." But those leaders lacked concern for the personalities beneath surface faithfulness. This precious couple finally understood that they found welcome only as givers of time and service but not as people who needed care and nurture.

It is important to see how an attitude of servant-leadership might have resulted in a more positive outcome.

1. A servant-leader seeks to build, not use people. Learn to listen carefully to your volunteers. If you pick up a sense that someone feels merely used, pursue it. Find out the particulars. The goal is mutual ministry, not one-way service.

2. Spend regular time with your volunteers and plan into your ministry structure the means for casual and informal conversations so you know them before the crises hit. In very large churches, of course, this work will necessarily be spread out, but it is an essential part of the pastoring process. Peterson writes:

> Pastoral work . . . is that aspect of Christian ministry that specializes in the ordinary. It is the nature of pastoral life to be attentive to, immersed in, and appreciative of the everyday texture of people's lives—the buying and selling, the visiting and meeting, the going and coming. There are also crisis events to be met: birth and death, conversion and commitment, baptism and Eucharist, despair and celebration. These also occur in people's lives and, therefore, in pastoral work. But not as everyday items.[1]

3. Stay on the lookout for growth opportunities for your volunteers. It may be hard to lose them from a position in which they perform comfortably and competently, but boredom is a powerful demotivator. A little change, a new challenge, the opportunity to learn a new skill—each may open whole new areas of ministry opportunities.

One woman had a respectable singing voice but did not know how to read music so had never joined the choir. The choir director offered to take the time to teach her. As her skills grew, so did her confidence that she had something to contribute. To that point, she had always stayed in the background, but within a year she began leading a women's Bible study group and became active in the church's mothers'-day-out program. When the directorship of that program was offered her, she willingly accepted the responsibility and turned it into a thriving ministry. She now faces the world rejoicing in the gifts God gave her, because someone took the time to be a part of her life when he taught her to read music.

All people need the sense of working together in groups. Research on group dynamics can help church leaders. Key features in a team or group include its reason for being, the sense of a common purpose, freedom to speak and participate, a sense of acceptance, respect from co-workers, opportunities to participate in decisions and in leadership, a clear understanding of what is expected, adequate equipping and training, accountability for performance, and effective communication.

Team members need to feel accepted and made a part of the group. People feel accepted when they are given opportunity to participate fully and when leaders listen to their ideas and suggestions. Participatory decision making, rather than authoritarian control, enhances this acceptance. Sharing the leadership role demonstrates the leader's confidence in volunteers and facilitates teamwork.

In a church with only one paid staff member (the pastor), that leader needs to accent participation of lay leaders in all ministry programs. This is true for churches with multiple staff as well. That was the genius of the New Testament church throughout the Book of Acts, and particularly at Antioch (Acts 11). When volunteers feel they are pawns in the pastor's program, work may get done quite adequately. However, that climate does not provide for leadership development, but merely the accomplishment of ministry tasks.

Mission Statement

Chapter 1 mentions the church's mission statement, but a brief reference fits here as well. All workers need to know and understand this statement and how their service fits into the total ministry of the church. Even the smallest job contributes. When people recognize that their ministry helps fulfill the purpose of the church, they discover that they have become a vital part of its ministry. Just *knowing* the mission statement is not enough; it must be *accepted* by volunteers, which results in a common purpose for ministry. Without this understanding and acceptance, teamwork will not develop.

Team Relationships

Team relationships are enhanced when people know what is expected of them. This is best done through careful explanation of the task, with adequate training. Too often leaders get so concerned about filling positions that they neglect the training people need to serve effectively. It is much better to prepare a worker for effective service through training and supervision than to be disappointed in performance because the volunteer does not know how to perform the work. Accountability comes when workers know what is expected of them and they have been given the equipment necessary to fulfill the task.

Developing an effective ministry team includes a clearly defined dream, a setting in which people feel free to risk their ideas and opinions, a sense of cooperation rather than competition, and a commitment to goals. Notice that this requires inclusion of all personnel in the total ministry all the way from the dream to the evaluation of the final result. Integrate individual suggestions from the group into the planning process to produce an effective team effort.

A positive team spirit among workers produces greater commitment to the ministry, less absenteeism, greater longevity in service, and people who are ful-filled in ministry. More on this in chapter 8.

Team Concept

This team concept cannot be built by people merely working together. It requires a significant time com-mitment. Their coming together regularly for planning meetings is a beginning. At these meetings they can pray for each other as well as for those special needs of people in the ministry. They work on plans for Sun-day's teaching session and develop significant learning activities. Meaningful friendships should be developed outside the regular teaching preparation times as well. All these elements facilitate a positive team.

Some leaders need to be convinced that a team approach to ministry is both practical and scriptural. Jethro's advice to Moses, when he found him judging the people from morning to evening, was that he share the task with capable men who were God-fearing and trustworthy (Exod. 18:13–26). Moses could not handle the task alone, and neither can you. Notice Moses did take Jethro's advice and selected capable people who shared the work.

A pastor informed his elders that the amount of time he spent counseling parishioners took time away from his other responsibilities such as preparing ser-mons, working with church boards and committees, and ministering to people in need. One of the elders, a trained school counselor, offered to assist him with the counseling load. The pastor responded by saying that the people wanted *him* to deal with their needs, not someone else. This sounds much like the Moses dilemma of overwork coupled with a lack of willing-ness to share the ministry.

John R. Cionca provides good insight when he suggests that a church leader can be compared to the manager of a sports team. The leader must work with the cooperative efforts of a team of players, and ministry can only be done effectively by using the skills of the whole team.[3] It is true that people can do more when they work together as a team than they can accomplish individually, no matter how hard they may work.

To carry the sports analogy a little further, notice what management expert W. Steven Brown says about the legendary football coach, Vince Lombardi. Brown was particularly interested in Lombardi because his surveys of managers indicated that many people considered the Green Bay coach the world's greatest manager.

> Think about how Lombardi managed. In NFL football, the coach cannot cross the sideline and move onto the playing field. He works in advance of playing time and on the side of the action. Before the game he prepares his players by anticipating the problems they will face and by readying them to meet those problems. He trains, advises, and encourages, but he never touches the ball. The coach cannot do the players' work for them.[4]

Brown goes on to suggest this as a model for effective fathers, but it will also work in a ministry which aims to pastor and equip church members.

Cooperation is the central ingredient of team ministry. Teamwork can only be achieved through voluntary effort pooled in a common sense. A helpful article entitled "About Building Morale" offers this significant paragraph:

> Cooperation must be practiced by everyone, by those who are supervising as well as by those who are supervised. It is a voluntary thing, a two-way street, a way of

living in which people work together to get something done. A fair index of a person's efficiency and management is the degree of working together that exists in his unit of the factory or office.[5]

Utilize Motivational Factors

Motivation means to activate, direct, and sustain interest in activities that lead to the achievement of a goal. Note the three parts of this definition. First, the person's initial interest must be secured. Then comes the direction in how to proceed. Finally, the person must maintain continuing interest in the process for long-term value to the organization. Obviously, in church ministry you need people who will not only stay on the job but will also continue in their ministry with excitement, purpose, and fulfillment.

Commitment to Ministry

This commitment to ministry is something every church desperately needs from its volunteers. Certainly, true motivation comes from God and is facilitated by the working of the Holy Spirit in their lives. Do not overlook this important spiritual dimension as you consider the motivation theory. In fact, this goes hand in hand with what prompts individuals to action when they seek to fulfill what God wants them to do with their lives.

Sometimes, however, volunteers are influenced more by the personality of a leader than by their desire to serve God in the church. That motivation for behavior is hardly desirable. Yes, leaders do influence followers, but true motivation for service in the church must come from God. The leader who can plant seeds of such motivation understands the factors that will influence individuals to action.

A motivational factor is anything that prompts people to act or influences them to get involved. These factors activate internal motives which, in turn, trigger positive response. Note that *the motives reside inside the person.* Only when unleashed can they give rise to behavior directed toward a goal.

Motivational factors include such things as the following:

1. to achieve a certain standard of excellence
2. to gain attention or status from peers, a teacher, or a leader
3. group loyalty
4. to work for tangible rewards and/or punishment
5. competition
6. power
7. to follow rules and routine
8. pleasure or fun
9. to gain acceptance
10. affiliation
11. self-worth
12. self-esteem
13. to avoid anxiety

Experts tell us these factors can prompt people to action. Looking at the list we discover that most are appropriate for Christians, while others may be questionable. The motivational factors that activate internal motives to lead individuals to fulfill God's purpose are proper for believers. Those that elevate the ego and promote personal pride are suspect. The key will be to encourage those motives that bring biblical fulfillment to people.

Wise leaders know their teams so well that they can appeal to wholesome and biblical values those team members treasure. Then genuine motivation takes place.

When goals are set by the entire group, rather than by the leader alone, the factor of achieving a standard of excellence is activated when the goal is achieved because the volunteer participated in establishing the standard. The key is ownership.

The illustration given earlier about the woman who learned to read music visibly pictures how the factor of self-worth can arouse a motive and bring a greater commitment to ministry.

Intrinsic and Extrinsic Incentives

Motives are activated by incentives, both intrinsic (within the person) and extrinsic (outside the person). Intrinsic incentives are preferable because they link the task to the goal. People are willing to work on the successful completion of a project when it fulfills the broader goal of assisting the church in doing its work more efficiently. Response to the task is positive when people can see its contribution to the overall good of the ministry.

Extrinsic incentives usually have no functional relationship to the task at hand. Have you ever heard of a church giving students candy bars for learning Scripture verses? The reward does not relate to the task, but the system does appear to work. An intrinsic reward would be the use of those Scripture verses to share the gospel with another person or to provide comfort to someone who has experienced loss. The reward comes in the use, not in an artificial gift.

Sometimes it seems necessary to use extrinsic incentives to secure people's attention, but you must move to intrinsic incentives as soon as possible. A lasting interest is seldom maintained with extrinsic incentives.

People claim different motives for serving in the church. The main ones include positive relationships with peers and encouragement from leaders. People want the opportunity to be fulfilled in ministry rather than meet someone else's performance expectations. They need to own the vision of ministry and not just buy into the leader's dream. They long to work with people who practice and live what they teach, to be part of a ministry team whose leader allows them freedom in how they do their ministry, to take part in open interaction of ideas and effective communication. All this results in encouragement, affirmation, and support. The leader who helps satisfy these motivations for church ministry will keep workers fulfilled and reverse the problem of major turnover in ministry positions.

Demotivators come into play when the leader's concern seems to stem from self-interest rather than seeking the best for the volunteer. A perceived lack of integrity results in an immediate loss of interest. Too much on too few, letting volunteers flounder, aiming too high, aiming too low, and insufficient recognition can be demotivational and contribute to resignations and/or a poor quality of ministry.

Over ten years ago *Leadership Journal* claimed that motivating and sustaining active participation of lay members in the church was a pastor's major problem. Undoubtedly those statistics have changed little during the past decade. Win Arn says, "The more members that become involved in church ministry roles, the easier it is to find the right persons best qualified and gifted for a particular ministry. Unfortunately, history shows that without an intentional priority and effective plan, those churches never reach these realistic possibilities."[6]

Application Activities

1. Evaluate the communication channels in your church. How do people know what is happening in the church's ministry? How do they find out about special events and programs? List the various communication channels and then evaluate their effectiveness. Ask workers to contribute to this evaluation.

2. From the above exercise, list and implement some effective ways that communication in your church can be improved.

3. To what extent do workers in your church get involved in the planning of activities that they will eventually implement? Do workers feel a part of the process? How does this principle facilitate good communication in the church?

4. Analyze the decision-making process in your church. Are workers involved in the process from the beginning or are they merely brought in to "rubber stamp" decisions already made by the leaders?

5. What opportunities do you provide for face-to-face communication in your church? Are they adequate? Do you need to develop more opportunities?

6. Review the elements that describe good teamwork: a reason for being, the sense of a common purpose, the freedom to speak and participate, the sense of acceptance, respect from co-workers, opportunities to participate in decisions and in leadership, a clear understanding of what is expected, adequate equipping and training, accountability for performance, and effective communication. How is your church accom-

plishing these elements with the workers? Do you have the sense of teamwork described in this chapter?

7. What can you do to facilitate better teamwork in your church?

8. What church teamwork lesson can you find in the illustration of Moses and Jethro? Does the do-it-all-yourself factor dominate your church? If so, what can be done to alleviate the problem?

9. How would you measure commitment to ministry among the volunteers in your church? Is this commitment based upon a desire to serve God or is it tied more to an individual leader's influence?

10. What motives keep people in your church on the job? Which of these are compatible with a spiritual desire to serve God? Which are not?

11. What incentives could you introduce that would be more intrinsic than extrinsic?

6

Training and Equipping Volunteers

Kevin, the leader of a minichurch (sometimes called flock or care group or household), had assessed his present membership and looked for someone to take it over. He really didn't want to give up the group. He and his wife had started it two years before, and it had grown into a warm and caring fellowship of believers. However, the time had come to divide it and make room for new people to join. Kevin would go with the new group. Its leader had no experience and had requested support for the first year. So after some time in prayer and consultation with the pastoral staff, Kevin asked Robert to consider taking the existing group.

Although Robert had served in this fellowship only three years, he showed evidence of Christian maturity. Eagerly he accepted the responsibility. He seemed confident he could continue the ministry. He mentioned that he deeply loved teaching and so would especially enjoy that part of his responsibility.

At that time, the congregation had no program to train its minichurch leaders. Many leaders had held their positions for some time and seemed to be handling them well. Everyone assumed Robert would do the same.

After a year and a half, Robert's minichurch disintegrated. He had been so eager to impart Bible knowledge to his group that he often spent over an hour lecturing in a monotone voice. He failed to provide adequate time for group bonding, fellowship, fun times, worship, and prayer. The fringe members quickly faded, but the faithful core hung in as long as possible. No one wanted to hurt Robert's feelings, so excuses for poor attendance became more creative.

After the damage was done, Kevin conferred with the pastoral staff. The analysis: "We assumed Robert knew what he was doing. He expressed such eagerness to take the job and never asked for help. He indicated that he had led groups before. We thought he would understand the need for balanced group time. We also thought he knew how to teach adults and understood their need to participate in Bible study, not just hear lectures. The failure of the group was not his fault. We never thought to train him."

Large corporations invest great sums of money and time in the training of workers. They know that for people to be successful they must know what is expected of them. Businesses do not develop new programs without adequately training their personnel.

Church leaders often overlook this approach. They develop a vision for a ministry and charge ahead without asking important preparatory questions. They usually expect workers to know, without training, how to perform a certain ministry.

In the 1990s churches are trying different strategies such as evening Sunday schools, small-group programs, boys' and girls' clubs, mothers'-day-out ministries, Bible studies, support groups, and many more. These ideas work successfully in churches across the land, but implementing them in your church takes more than an idea or a wish.

Several basic questions must be addressed: Why is training necessary? Who develops training programs? Who does the training? How much training is necessary? When can the training be scheduled? What materials are available for training?

Why Is Training Necessary?

On the surface, this appears an unnecessary question. Most will agree that people need to understand what to do and how to do it, regardless of the ministry opportunity. From interviews and observations, however, it appears that church leaders do not provide adequate training for their volunteers.

Yes, sometimes leaders might give a brief description of the job to a potential worker and perhaps even provide resource materials. Unfortunately, this is often as far as it goes. Like Robert, many workers are left alone to figure out what is expected and how to fulfill the responsibility. When this happens, volunteers commonly determine their own activities and establish minimal acceptable performance standards.

To Coordinate the Educational Program

Consider children's church programs. Churches ask people to serve in this major responsibility and sometimes provide them with a book or a kit of materials. Leaders assume that, from these meager resources, people can develop a quality hour of learning activities. The usual measure of success is whether or not they can keep the children occupied without making too much noise or disrupting the adult worship service.

But how can proper training enhance this potential educational and worship experience? For one thing, the workers must know what other experiences the children have on any given Sunday. What did they study in Sunday school? What other experiences, such as music, recreation, and refreshments are included? How long have they been at church? This information is necessary to plan a coordinated educational and worship experience. A planning and training time with all of the workers of the various ministries for children on a Sunday morning will help to accomplish this.

To Use Resources Effectively

In addition to knowing about other ministries, volunteers need to know how to use their materials and resources effectively. Publishers develop fine materials for various ministries, but if people do not use them properly, the educational experience will come up short. In fact, most complaints about curricular materials really deal with the way people use them. This should not be a surprise, for some researchers report that many children's Sunday school teachers spend thirty minutes or less in preparation time each week. Yes, sometimes the curricular materials are weak, and when this happens the problem needs to be corrected. But first, see if your teachers are handling them properly.

Today many educators emphasize life-span development or an understanding of age characteristics. Volunteers must have a good understanding of the developmental stages of the people they serve. Teachers who have taught a certain age group for a period of time learn some of this information by observation, but excellent resources are available and a good training program should include their use.

To Provide a Quality Product

How foolish it would be to suggest that the type of "product" the church produces is of no interest. As salt and light to the world, Christians want to entice people to Christ, not repel them. This leads to an interesting balancing act: the need to develop people, with all their foibles and failures, and the need to attract an increasingly sophisticated world. A business organization seeking to develop a superior product will look for the top available personnel with skills for the presenting task. The church, however, has a different work force available. Edward R. Dayton and Ted W. Engstrom call the church both the most sophisticated and the most difficult organization to manage. They explain it this way:

> This organization, by definition, accepts the "walking wounded" along with the skilled and unskilled. Imagine how you would feel if one day there were a knock at the door of the business you were managing. Outside are four men carrying another on a stretcher. Their friend is deaf and dumb and physically incapacitated but "loves the Lord and wants to be a member of your organization." What would you do with such a person? He doesn't fit any job description that you have anywhere. The manager of any organization with the sole purpose of accomplishing a task could only say "Sorry" and send the person away. Yet that is the

dilemma faced by the pastor (manager) of the local church.[1]

But the church is different. Precisely because we maintain an open door—whosoever will may come—the church offers to the world assurances that all those "whosoever wills" be offered a place of ministry. Leaders who seek to set up programs that effectively help believers mature and draw a lost world to Christ may find it helpful to take some hints from W. Edwards Deming. This genius who revitalized Japanese industry directed the changes that caused "made in Japan" to be known as a symbol of quality instead of a symbol of shoddiness.

As he refined his philosophy of management, he consolidated his material into "Fourteen Points" and "Seven Deadly Diseases," which he taught for more than three decades. Not all of them are applicable to a church situation, but the implementation of those which are could have a powerful impact on the production of a quality ministry. For congregations, the following principles seem most useful:

> *Improve constantly and forever the system of production and service.* Improvement is not a one-time effort. Management is obligated to continually look for ways to reduce waste and improve quality.
>
> *Institute training.* Too often, workers have learned their jobs from another worker who was never trained properly. They are forced to follow unintelligible instructions. They can't do their jobs because no one tells them how.
>
> *Institute leadership.* The job of a supervisor is not to tell people what to do or to punish them but to lead. Leading consists of helping people do a bet-

ter job and of learning by objective methods who is in need of individual help.

Drive out fear. Many employees are afraid to ask questions or to take a position, even when they do not understand what the job is or what is right or wrong. People will continue to do things the wrong way, or to not do them at all. The economic [or spiritual] loss from fear is appalling. It is necessary for better quality and productivity that people feel secure.

Break down barriers between staff areas. Often staff areas—departments, units, whatever—are competing with each other or have goals that conflict. They do not work as a team so they can solve or foresee problems. Worse, one department's goals may cause trouble for another.

Remove barriers to pride of workmanship. People are eager to do a good job and distressed when they can't. Too often, misguided supervisors, faulty equipment, and defective materials stand in the way. These barriers must be removed.

Institute a vigorous program of education and retraining. Both management and the workforce will have to be educated in the new methods, including teamwork.

Take action to accomplish the transformation. It will take a special top management team with a specific plan of action to carry out the quality mission. Workers can't do it on their own, nor can managers.[2]

Deming goes on to say that lack of constancy of purpose, an emphasis on short-term results, and management mobility are three means to kill the goal of quality.

Who Develops Training Programs?

If we agree that people need training to accomplish their ministry tasks effectively, the next step is to determine who handles the training programs.

Usually churches utilize different groups to head their various programs. A music or worship committee may plan for the worship services. They might also oversee the various music and worship activities such as choirs, special music, drama presentations, and worship planning. Training opportunities may include choir and ensemble rehearsals, learning to read music, vocal lessons, instrumental lessons, drama instruction, worship planning, reading Scripture, making announcements, and leading worship.

The Christian education committee usually takes responsibility for the educational ministries of the church, including Sunday school, youth programs, boys' and girls' clubs, children's church, vacation Bible schools, Bible studies, small-group ministries, men's and women's ministries, mothers'-day-out programs. Each of these ministries requires training for their leaders. Other church ministries have similar groups or individuals that oversee their programs.

The philosophy of ministry we have been advancing implies that all the ministry groups have a clear understanding of how their particular service contributes to the total church strategy and its mission statement. When this is clear, each group or individual plans training experiences in cooperation, not in competition, with other ministries. This includes a synchronized schedule of training events and programs, a cooperative balance in the recruitment of possible workers, and a sincere appreciation for ministries other than their own. Certainly all those responsible for a particular ministry have some responsibility for developing a plan for training, though they may not do the training themselves.

Effective training programs do more than just teach basic skills. If we really want to develop group leaders, we need serious programs aimed at precisely that. Paul G. Hiebert writes:

> Training leaders is a more difficult task for we must train them to think and to make decisions on their own. But this is threatening, for it means that they can and must challenge our own beliefs and plans. Key to the process is to teach them to critique what we ourselves have taught. There is no ego trip involved in this. Rather, we expect in the end to be set aside as new leaders take over, teach new ideas and set new courses of action.[3]

Who Does the Training?

The supervisory committee or board is responsible to develop plans for the training of workers. Who, then, does the actual training?

Ministry Committee Members

Certainly someone from the responsible committee can lead the training sessions. In fact, this is a good way to demonstrate that the committee maintains a genuine interest in the ministry. If they really know what needs to be done, they can lead the volunteers in the best way to do it.

Church Staff

Church staff members can also do the training. A careful analysis of the role of the church staff leads us to believe that one of their primary tasks is to equip God's people for ministry (Eph. 4:11–13). This passage offers a New Testament manifesto, a biblical declaration of intent or policy. Church staffs need to be dedicated to the development of lay workers, to equip, enable and empower them.

Program Director

Directors of the various programs should have a good understanding of what needs to be done. One valuable principle (decentralization) states that training should be done by the person closest to the ministry and who knows the most about it. For example, a departmental Sunday school superintendent should, if possible, train teachers in her own department. This approach, however, does not relieve the supervising committee from the overall responsibility to see that training takes place.

Outside Expert

Sometimes, to bring visibility to a training experience, churches bring in outside consultants to provide motivation, challenge the workers, and provide some basic training. A church choir may bring in a clinician to lead them for a weekend retreat during which they work on vocal techniques, improving the ensemble, diction, interpretation, and future music presentations. Most choir directors can and will do this themselves, but bringing in a specialist provides a distinctive commitment to a quality choir ministry.

Educational workers from other churches in the area who specialize in certain age groups are another source of trainers for a church. In fact, one helpful training experience is to visit a church that has an effective ministry and to watch its leaders model a program.

If there is a Bible college, Christian college, or theological seminary nearby, professors or advanced students are a good resource for a training program. Some schools provide evening training classes for lay people both on campus and in local churches. Consider hosting classes in your church so your workers can take advantage of the opportunity.

Conventions and Conferences

Regional Sunday school and Christian ministries conventions provide an excellent source of training opportunities. Usually programs are set up in tracks that offer multiple workshops for people who work with certain age groups or other ministries. This arrangement allows for several specialized training sessions in a given conference. Outstanding workshop leaders and speakers are brought in from across the country and provide encouragement, motivation, specialized training, an update on resources, and fellowship with others who serve in Christian ministries in area churches.

But the most effective training for the people in your church is that which you design and carry out locally. Usually the broader the outside training experience, the less likely it will meet the specific needs of your workers. A program designed in your church can address your particular needs and will be much more effective.

How Much Training Is Necessary?

Different ministry opportunities require varying levels of training. Some ministries may require only a session or two, while others, such as leading inductive Bible studies, will require ongoing training.

Each ministry should establish its minimal acceptable amount of training necessary and then work to achieve this standard before someone is placed in a position of service.

Who makes these decisions? The supervising committee or board establishes the guidelines and works to see them implemented.

Listing of Ministry Opportunities

Look back at the listing of ministry opportunities included on the church ministry survey in chapter 3. Under each of the ministries on your list indicate what training will enable people to serve effectively. Be sure to consider a person's past experience as well as current needs for training.

For example, under the listing for education you will find "Teach Adults." What training should you require for this important position? The first task is to develop a job description for this teaching position. The items in this description will reveal their own training requirements. For example, you might come up with the following:

Adult teachers must:
    be Christians
    know the Scriptures
    know that the ministry of teaching is God-ordained
    live for the Lord and grow in their Christian experience
    be good communicators
    know how to teach adults effectively
    know the needs of the learners
    be faithful in their teaching responsibility
    be willing to participate in training opportunities

know the approved curriculum and how to use it
effectively

participate in the outreach opportunities of the
class

spend time in fellowship opportunities with class
members

Preparation of Job Descriptions

Some elements of the job description do not require special training, such as being a Christian. This is a prerequisite to all Bible teaching. The elements listed as "know" do. How can we determine if a person *knows* the Scriptures, *knows* how to teach adults, and *knows* the needs of the learners? In these areas, we want teachers to continually grow. We expect that they will know more of the Scriptures each year and will improve in their teaching and in the understanding of adult needs.

All adult teachers should be expected to participate in a set amount of training each year, and this training should provide enrichment in the "know" areas.

Job Description Outline

Position Title:_____

Position Purpose: (How does this person serve the overall mission of the organization?)

Description of Function: (In a sentence or two describe the position.)

Qualification/Specifications: (What qualities and competencies are required for this position?)

Responsibilities: (List major duties separately, using descriptive verbs like *direct, implement,* etc.)

1.

2.

3.

4.

5.

6.

7.

8.

Accountability to: (Identify office of immediate supervisor.)

Accountability for: (Identify subordinates by position.)

Committee Memberships: (List committees and indicate which, if any, must be chaired.)

Goals for 19_____: (Reviewed and revised annually.)

Churches often require a minimum of one training experience a year, such as a seminar, workshop, conference, or class. In addition, they recommend selected reading and observation of others teaching the same age group. Also, teachers should attend the regular planning or teachers' meetings of the church.

What motivates church volunteers to attend religious training programs? That's a question Fred Wilson asked in a significant research program developed in southern California just a few years ago. Readers interested in a full report of the study can check the endnote. But in summary Wilson said this:

> Motivation to participate in adult religious training has more than one focus. In addition to the desire to be trained for ministry, there are strong motivations towards receiving help in personal spiritual growth through the ministry of God's Word as well as cognitive input. This should influence how the events are promoted as well as the extent to which each should be part of the training event.[4]

When Can the Training be Scheduled?

Requirements should be set for training ministry throughout the church, but if people cannot find the time to attend training sessions, the entire concept will fail. Here we need a "reality check." People are busy. They already give of their time to serve on a regular basis. Somehow we must find ways to accomplish the needed training without destroying already busy schedules.

One solution is to see if people are involved in too many ministries. Since each ministry will require some training, scheduling for those involved in several will be more complicated. Limiting the number of ministry commitments should open up some time for training.

Look at the church calendar and schedule. Can you provide training when people are already at church? People will appreciate a consolidated schedule rather than to have to make a special trip back to the church.

A one-session training time for adult Sunday school class officers could be held just prior to the class. It could also be held during the regular Sunday school hour if we can provide substitutes for that day. Ron Held commends the use of the Sunday school hour for training volunteers.

> Most of them will already be there, so you would not have to schedule another night. Set up a series of short-term courses, six to eight weeks, organized on the basis of your current need for workers, such as altar workers, boys or girls program leaders and Sunday school teachers.[5]

Ongoing training may be more difficult to schedule, so try to offer it in conjunction with other meetings. Sometimes the Sunday school hour is best. Sunday or Wednesday evenings are some other possibilities. One church had a number of shift workers, so they scheduled their training time at midnight, when the workers from second shift could come. Others utilize early morning meetings. Use your creativity and come up with the time when most people can participate.

Home study offers yet another possibility. Books, videos, and other resources are available for nearly every kind of ministry. Leaders can provide these to the workers on a check-out basis and encourage their use.

The effort to consolidate meetings at the church does not suggest the elimination of other meetings.

There is no substitute for regular planning meetings for ministry groups such as Sunday school workers, boys' and girls' club workers, youth workers, and all other ministry volunteers.

What Materials Are Available?

Nearly every church ministry has resources for teaching and training workers. Publishing houses produce many high-quality training materials. Denominations, parachurch organizations, and schools develop and publish resources. The question is not availability but which materials best meet the needs.

The first place to contact for training materials for a given ministry is the national or local office of that ministry. If you use Sunday school curriculum materials, then call the publisher or the local representative and ask for their recommendations. This way the training experience will parallel the materials being taught.

If your church needs specialized training experiences, go through catalogues from publishers and contact local Christian bookstores for help. You will be pleasantly surprised with the amount of material available for every kind of ministry. Contact professors at Christian colleges and seminaries. Many schools have curriculum labs which display many of the resources.

Churches should consider developing a learning-resources center for volunteers so that the training materials will be available on a check-out basis to those who need them. Include a basic Bible-and-theology library with specialized areas in Christian education, counseling, marriage and family, etc. Also secure magazines, tapes, and videos. The director of the center should get materials into the hands of the workers by offering to supplement what they are presently teaching. This takes extra time in study and research, but the benefits are worth the effort.

Meanwhile, the unresolved problem of Robert remains and of his leaders who concluded, "We never thought to train him." Review the story of Kevin and Robert as you answer some of the questions of this chapter. Who should have developed that training program? Who should have done the training? How much training did Robert really need? When might that training have been scheduled? Volunteers are the lifeblood of church ministry. Don't lose any of them to defective or invisible training programs.

Application Activities

1. Answer honestly: What programs or strategies has your church introduced recently that did not provide adequately for the training of the workers who were to lead the programs? What is presently happening to these ministries? What can be done at this time to correct the problems?

2. According to this chapter (and from your own understanding), why is it necessary to train workers in church ministry?

3. Assuming there was an affirmative answer to question 2, who should take the lead in developing and scheduling training programs for the various church ministries?

4. Where do you find the teachers and leaders for the needed training programs? What is the basic principle to follow in finding the best teachers for training?

5. How can churches determine how much training is necessary for certain leadership positions?

6. With everyone's busy schedules, when can training experiences be scheduled for church workers?

Develop your answer from your own church schedule, using some of the suggestions in this chapter.

7. How do you find the resources for these important training experiences?

8. What commitment will you make to see that proper training is provided for the volunteer positions in your church? How can you get other church leaders to accept this commitment as well?

7

Supervising Volunteers

Barbara, always enthusiastic and uniquely able to give her services almost full-time as a volunteer, had a vision—a women's ministry that encompassed all the needs and talents of the women in her church and enabled them to reach far and wide into the community. She listed her goals: serious Bible studies with highly trained teachers, emotional support groups for those who had been domestically or otherwise abused, structured mentoring of the younger women by the older women, a care or mercy ministry for those who were hurting financially or dealing with serious illness in the immediate family, holiday parties for underprivileged children, and a series of Saturday luncheons for women who held full-time jobs and tended to feel estranged from the usual women's activities.

The church gave her the green light. Go for it!

Eight years later, exhausted and burned out, Barbara complained to a friend of many years as they talked over a cup of coffee, "If I don't do the work, it never gets done. People say they'll do something, but they don't follow through. I spend so much time running around, setting up programs, propping things up, teaching Bible studies. Even worse, after we've set something up, we'll get bumped by another church activity that needs the same space."

Her friend responded, "Barbara, how much contact do you have with the pastoral staff person who delegated all these responsibilities to you?"

"Almost none. He's an assistant pastor and we meet once a year to go over my budget requests. Every once in a while he'll ask how things are going. He has indicated that he is too busy to worry about my program and has lots of confidence that I can handle this on my own."

Another question from her friend: "Do you meet regularly with the women whom you've asked to carry certain responsibilities? What is your organizational structure?"

"I have an advisory board I meet with whenever I feel like calling a meeting, about four or five times a year. However, none of them actually take responsibility for any programs or activities. The organizational structure is just me, I guess."

One final question from her friend: "Barbara, has anyone ever given you loving supervision over your work, or taught you how to supervise others?"

"I'm really not sure what you mean."

Churches and Christian leaders increasingly struggle to find quality workers like Barbara who can fulfill various tasks of ministry. Society's changes in recent decades underscore significant difficulties in this effort. Nearly every church leader knows that the most significant challenge facing congregations is recruiting busy people for ministry and then supervising them.

Effective supervision can determine whether or not programs and strategies rest upon biblical responsibility to meet significant needs. Without this understanding, ministries may become mere programs with no obvious rationale. To repeat, people respond more to ministry opportunities that are part of a broader church strategy rather than isolated, personal ministry efforts that do not contribute to an overall purpose.

After we set biblical foundations, discover needs, and establish ministry goals and strategies, we can begin to understand the importance of supervision. As we teach the use of spiritual gifts, coupled with practical and administrative suggestions to assist Christian leaders and workers, the church can sense the opportunity to fulfill its mission.

The church belongs to the Lord, and ministry is under his control. Scripture calls us to serve him through the church, and as leaders, to equip people for service in ministry. If God helps us develop strategies or programs for ministry, he will also guide us in supervising the volunteers who staff them.

On rare occasions God may choose to supply workers as he supplied manna from heaven for the people of Israel in the wilderness. But even they had to go out and collect it. Usually he expects us to be proactive in the finding, recruiting, training, and placing of workers in ministry. Then we cannot ignore the essential ongoing role of supervisory leadership.

Foundational Principles of Supervision

Ministries Must Reflect the Mission Statement

People respond to opportunities when they see how the suggested ministry contributes to the overall objectives of the church. An earlier chapter emphasized that too often these statements are unavailable and people are not given the opportunity to see them in print. Yet supervision is inseparably related to objectives, and objectives must be based upon the church's mission statement.

A mission statement helps people understand the nature and purpose of the church. It should cover worship, evangelism, education, fellowship, and ministry. Every ministry in which a church engages must be evaluated on the basis of how well its workers handle these areas. As workers are supervised and affirmed, they can be reminded of the mission statement and how their specific activity contributes to the total ministry of the church.

Ministries Must Be Based On the Needs of People

Once a church knows what God wants it to do (mission statement), it can work at its achievement (needs assessment). To find the needs, look both inside and outside the church. Today many talk about the importance of a need-based church ministry. People are more likely to respond to something if they feel it will meet their needs. These needs, however, must be based on God's Word and not just the whims and desires of people.

Christian workers look for their needs to be met in their ministries. But more likely, their Christian love motivates them to be sensitive to and meet the needs of others. How effectively are your workers' needs being met? More important, how well are they meeting the needs of people they serve?

People Respond to Ministry Goals and Strategies

Goals are developed from the mission statement and the church's awareness of needs. Goals can also provide an important challenge. People often respond to goals they perceive will fulfill a desirable objective. True servants of the Lord find joy in serving the Savior in ways the Spirit has gifted them. When strategies emerge from goals, they meet the needs and God's purpose for the church. Personal fulfillment comes from knowing that what you are doing is important and in line with what God expects.

Ask if the program's strategies are designed to most efficiently and effectively reach its goals. Are the workers' understandings and practices compatible with those strategies? Do adjustments need to be made on paper and in practice?

Organizational Principles of Supervision

Scripture records many events in which proper administrative principles were used. Remember that these events took place prior to the present-day management movement. The spiritual gift of administration (1 Cor. 12:28) underscores the importance God gives to doing ministry in the best possible way.

Yes, ministry can become bogged down with an overabundance of administrative structure and regulations. When this happens, people lose sight of the biblical purpose of what they are doing and focus only on unrelated procedures and requirements. This is wrong, but when ministry is performed without proper planning, then that is wrong, too. Administrative procedures assist people to minister properly and effectively. But when they get in the way, they are out of place.

People Respond to Supervisors Who Plan Ahead

Good planning must include forecasting, establishing objectives, programming, scheduling, budgeting, and establishing policies and procedures. These things do not just happen. Leaders carefully invest time and energy in these activities so that the programs can be carried on effectively. This gives direction to the ministry and motivates workers to be involved. It frustrates volunteer workers when things are not well planned. They feel that if they give their time to the church, the church, in turn, should have plans and resources to do things properly and effectively.

Do your workers know the plans for the ministry's future, understand them, agree with them? Do they feel rewarded for their time? Any hints of their spending inordinate amounts of time or too little time on their ministries? Are they satisfied with their physical equipment, educational materials, training?

People Respond to Supervisors Who Are Organized

Organization involves structure, delegation, and establishment of relationships. It makes it possible for people to work together in the task of ministry. Structure provides the practical framework of an organization and permits workers to see how their ministries fit with the overall design or the whole church's task of ministry. Successful leaders have learned to delegate tasks. When people see one person doing all the work, they "check out" of the ministry and let that person do it.

Do workers feel the work is evenly or fairly distributed? Do they readily accept responsibilities? Any hint that individuals are assuming work overloads or allowing themselves to be dumped on? Any workers becoming dead wood or feeling left out? Does someone have a problem articulating needs or frustrations? Do you give workers opportunity to blow their own horns, to vent their enthusiasm over their successes?

People Respond to Supervisors Who Share Their Vision

Emerging leaders must be involved in decision making, communicating, motivating, selecting, and developing people in ministry. When you encourage volunteers to participate in these functions, the ministries become theirs rather than yours. When leaders frequently talk about "my" ministry, they verbally deny this important principle.

Yes, leaders must have vision, but that vision can be developed from a shared perspective, rather than in solo fashion. Shared vision enhances group motivation. Also, when people share in the planning, they know more about the strategy to use.

Evaluate yourself. Are you a good listener? Do your workers confide in you, feel free to make suggestions? Can you accept suggestions, criticism, praise? Can you discuss options with your workers, make compromises, come to agreements? Do your workers feel you understand them? Do they empathize with you? Do they feed you as well as each other?

People Respond to Supervisors Who Evaluate Their Work

Evaluation is an important but often neglected part of ministry. People may be threatened and not want to serve if they think someone is always checking on them. You need to emphasize that evaluation helps people improve their service. It never aims to punish those who serve.

Standards for assessment must be set prior to the evaluation time. It is inappropriate when Sunday school teachers are observed for the purpose of evaluation when they are not told ahead of time what the evaluator is looking for.

Whatever we ask people to do in ministry must have clearly written objectives, which become the standard for evaluation. If volunteers and their supervisors establish objectives together, wider "ownership" is likely, and the task will probably be performed effectively. People will be willing to submit to this kind of assessment because they have had a part in designing it.

One major aspect of evaluation is debriefing. Evaluation measures workers' effectiveness against the objectives mutually agreed upon at the beginning. Debriefing brings the supervisor and the volunteer face to face to discuss what went right, what went wrong, and how the ministry can be improved in the future.

People respond to supervisors who demonstrate genuine care and concern. Often people get the impression that church leaders are only interested in them for what they can contribute to the advancement or preservation of church programs. But discipleship means being interested in people for themselves.

Not all supervisor meetings go smoothly. Sometimes the volunteer refuses to take suggestions and is dissatisfied with your evaluation or recommendations. The first thing to do when this happens is to determine the cause. Is it a personality clash? Does the volunteer disagree with the overall philosophy of ministry? What is the volunteer really saying by these actions? If the cause is a basic misunderstanding, then a solution is close at hand. If, however, the cause is absolute disagreement and even hostility, the problem must be addressed and dealt with appropriately.

Do not ignore these problems because they will only get larger. Talk directly to the individual and try to resolve the differences. If this does not work, consider moving the volunteer to another position. Perhaps the problem was misplacement in a ministry position. It may be necessary to dismiss the volunteer, and if it comes to this, be sure you consult with others to confirm this tactic. People know when they are not doing a good job and when others around them are not responding to their ministry. Dealing with the problem directly, but with sensitivity, is the best approach, because you want the volunteer to learn and grow from the experience and you want the ministry to go forward as well.

Evaluation is not always a formal process. Actually evaluation is going on all the time. Observations, responses from those being ministered to, records, and ministry successes provide means for assessment. A good leader will take advantage of all of these informal opportunities.

Spiritual Principles of Supervision

Everyone can have an opportunity to serve, even though it may not be in a high-visibility, high-influence kind of position. Everyone who serves needs supervision, and the quality of that supervision may very well determine whether that person continues at a low level of ministry effectiveness or grows toward more responsible ministry roles.

In this book, we have tried to weave together the strands necessary for the recruitment and retention of lay workers in the church. We have touched on many things: the need for clearly understood mission statements, the model of servant leadership, the goals of ministries, the usefulness of administrative principles. We have emphasized the need to bring people along, to encourage them to accept and be trained for new ministry opportunities.

Scripture clearly indicates that no believer ever reaches the point where he or she functions alone. From the beginning, we were created to exist as part of a community, for "it is not good for the man to be alone" (Gen 2:18). Ephesians 4 presents the prime model: "From him [Christ] the whole body, joined and held together by every supporting ligament, grows and builds itself up in love, as each part does its work" (v. 16). Christians give to one another what they have to give, and they receive that which they lack, for they are not complete when they are alone.

Important to receiving that which people lack is their understanding of their need for supervision or accountability. Most people have difficulty evaluating their own work with any degree of objectivity. Often they tend either to devastating negativism ("I'm no good at this anyway, and I might as well quit") or swing to unrealistic optimism ("I'm good, and don't try to tell me otherwise").

Many have come to equate supervision with criticism, for that is their experience, and so shy away from any further exposure to it. However, whether or not supervision includes some negative feedback, the Scriptures remind us, "no discipline seems pleasant at the time, but painful. Later on, however, it produces a harvest of righteousness and peace for those who have been trained by it" (Heb. 12:11).

Do you sense in your church an air of excitement, of enthusiasm for God's work? Is the Holy Spirit moving through your church? Is there a spirit of mutual love of the Lord, an eagerness to build up the body, to bring God's love to all the members and to a hurting world? Is this spirit contagious, attracting those outside the body? Or is it a time of lull, of plodding without measurable progress? If so, are you willing to wait for the Lord's own good time? Can you practice prayerful patience while all of you do your best in what you believe God wants you to do? Then will you be ready for the Spirit's rich harvest of fruits on your labor when it does come?

Making It Happen

How can you learn to supervise and be supervised without unnecessary hurt and with the positive result of righteousness? Think about Barbara, the wonderfully talented and terribly burned-out women's ministry director. What did she need in the way of supervision? What did she need to give in supervising others? In a later conversation, her friend asked that very question and came up with this list to summarize Barbara's responses.

1. Barbara led a major ministry division in the church. Even though she was not a paid staff member, she needed to be a part of the regularly scheduled staff meetings to see how her ministry fit within the greater scope of the church's overall mission.

2. She wanted to know that accounts were kept short between her and her supervisor. In other words, when she did make mistakes or when correction was needed, she wanted to know about it immediately, deal with it, and then know it would not haunt her. She was aware of one case in the church when a list of mistakes and errors in judgment was kept over a period of three years and then presented on one devastating evening to the lay volunteer. The fear that it might happen encouraged her to keep her distance from those who were really there to help.

3. Barbara needed to be taught sound administrative principles. As with Robert (whose minichurch dissolved), the pastoral staff assumed she knew these

things. In this case, it seemed more likely that both the staff and the highly responsible lay leaders would have profited from a good seminar and a series of lessons on church management and people skills.

4. She needed someone to model for her the mentoring that she herself wanted to do for the women with whom she worked. It may have been necessary in her case to go outside her local church to find a woman who could adequately mentor her, but she was never encouraged to do so. Indeed, it was never mentioned as an option. In effect, she placed herself, with the blessing from the staff, in a nearly impossible situation. She was to set up a program and ministry she had neither seen nor experienced. Good supervision should have recognized this lack in her experience and sought to remedy it.

5. Barbara was very aware of her own tendency to underdelegate. A high-energy person, she often quickly lost patience with those who did not work as quickly as she. Because this destructive pattern was lifelong, she could not easily shed it. She needed to know that someone cared enough about her to confront her lovingly and honestly when she was hovering too closely or taking back already delegated tasks.

This should have been part of the training-supervising process, "speaking the truth in love" (Eph. 4:15). It required a high level of trust between Barbara and her supervisor. His hands-off style, which he thought expressed confidence, communicated indifference to her. It could be that he was not the appropriate person for this task, but at least he should have pointed out to her that she did need someone to do this for her and made sure Barbara received this kind of feedback.

6. Most important, Barbara needed to know her supervisor sincerely desired to see her grow in Christ, not just create an effective program. Her moments of worst discouragement came when she felt most alone,

that she didn't have a coach, so to speak, pulling for her all the way. She knew the women in her ministry profited from this type of support, but after a while she found herself unable to give it because her own reserves were not refilled. No one is exempt from the need to be pastored, and possibly ministry leaders need it most because of the enormous drain on their emotional energies. Effective and caring supervision would both recognize and supply that need.

In everything from elementary schools to professional football, we hear a lot about mastering the basics. In elementary school it may be essential reading skills; in football, blocking and tackling represent the basics. In supervision of volunteers, the basics include necessary information, clear objectives, effective evaluation, appreciation, and a climate of acceptance and caring. Engstrom and Dayton write:

> Most people respond to the expectation of their leaders. If the leader has high expectations of the person, so will that person. If the leader doesn't expect much, chances are neither will the person. Expectations are communicated through standards, descriptions of what is to be done and how it is to be done. This is one of the most difficult of management tasks. Good performance needs to be reinforced. Less than adequate performance needs to be noted and plans to correct it carried through. It takes time. It takes a *competent* manager![1]

Let's conclude this chapter by talking about Doug, a physician in a major metropolitan area who came to Christ as an adult in the early stages of his medical training. As his career responsibilities grew, so did his passion for Christ and his desire to have an effective ministry. He sharpened his teaching skills while working as a professor in a medical school. To translate the usefulness of that gift to the church, he attended graduate-level seminary classes in the evenings. Over the years, he volunteered his talents for medical missionary trips, taught a Sunday school class, and finally began to serve a term as elder.

Unfortunately, before his term expired, he and a number of other elders resigned and left the church. In conversation afterward, he explained some of his disillusionment.

"I found that the church wanted to use me and my money, but the pastoral staff was not interested in seeing me grow as a Christian. Our church was overflowing with talented men and women, but we had no direction, no goal, no purpose. If we could fit into the established programs, fine. If we had ideas for different ministries, we were given lip service to try them but no support, no encouragement, no backup. The message came through clearly: Stick with business as usual, even if that business had no effect on the surrounding community. I want to participate in a ministry that knows where it is going and why."

In the same conversation Pam, another member who had left, spoke up. "I know the church is not a business. Nonetheless, good management principles are gifts from God. Businesses without long-range planning make horrible work places. It's one scramble after another to make it work, leaving employees frustrated and unhappy. Our church functioned just like that—a series of disconnected programs, with no reasonably achievable goals or ways to measure our progress."

A third leader, an executive with an international corporation, added, "It seemed as though our pastoral staff would grab whatever crazy idea came their way for church growth without evaluating whether it was right for our church, our particular community, the gifts and talents available to us. They seemed to be more interested in making us fit their program than in discovering what we as lay leaders could envision happening in our church. I feel used, not nurtured."

A sad case, possibly extreme in its manifestations with so many lay leaders leaving at once, but the sentiments expressed by these frustrated people are not uncommon. Sometimes the church talks about developing lay leaders, but when those lay leaders actually assume serious responsibility for ministry, professional staff get nervous and even wish they would "stay in their place." No wise pastor would say this, of course, but actions that downplay development of lay leadership communicate precisely the attitudes that drove these good folks away from a church they loved and wanted to serve.

Application Activities

1. Review the six foundational principles listed in this chapter. Which of these principles does your church need to work on in the coming months? Outline the steps necessary to make certain that your congregation operates according to these important principles.

2. From the problems listed both in this chapter and in chapter 2, which ones need your immediate attention? Outline a strategy to deal with these problems in a realistic manner during the coming year.

3. List all the possible ways to supervise volunteers suggested in this chapter. Then identify which ones your church is using on a regular basis. From the list, which ones could you add to your ministry that would facilitate better supervision?

8

Keeping That Team
of Volunteers Vital

The job is yours, Dave. This is a big church because people are drawn by the superb preaching. However, we've developed a reputation for being cold and uncaring. I want you to design and implement a program which will turn our church into a warm and intimate fellowship again."

Although new to the church, Dave had experience in this particular area of ministry. He had successfully instituted programs to deal with this problem in two other organizations and kept on the latest research in the field. He also brought with him four important pieces of knowledge: (1) his confidence that what worked one place would not necessarily work somewhere else; (2) his own strengths—big picture planning and team development; (3) his own weaknesses—poor at details and follow-through; and (4) his absolute inability to do this task without a strong team.

Despite his eagerness to get things rolling, Dave spent the first year behind the scenes. He mapped out his plan and then worked on getting to know key people with whom he could share his goals. One by one he put together a team. He arranged for team members to spend some extended periods of time together, just to get to know one another. He taught them how to use assessment tools so they would better understand each other's working and relating styles. He modeled for them the program he hoped to implement in the entire church.

As he worked with these people, he continually modified his original plan. He took into account the strengths and weaknesses of people he had pulled together. He asked for their feedback, suggestions, dreams, and ideas. Together they tried to incorporate as much of this input as possible. As his team attempted to implement the program, they came back to the meetings knowing they were free to share the problems and frustrations they faced.

At the end of three years, a program was in place and functioning. Yes, they still needed to work out some bugs, but the team faced the challenges, confident they could count on one another for support and ideas. Dave never failed to give those people credit when someone commented on the changes taking place. He knew too well that it would never have happened without them. They had amply proved the truth of the statement, The whole is greater than the sum of its parts.

All that you have read so far could take years to complete in a struggling church. But remember, it began with the initial interview, an early step in recruitment strategy.

Building a ministry team requires closing the door on the high attrition of workers in volunteer ministry. After going to all the effort to find and enlist volunteers, it is very discouraging when they only serve a short time. How can we keep good people on the team? As Dave well understood, one of the key ways to keep people involved in ministry is to permit them to feel a sense of accomplishment and fulfillment in what they do. His experience can help us understand how to pull together a ministry team of volunteers who work together effectively.

Team Ministry Requires Effective Leadership

The imperialist leadership style of much contemporary Christianity holds no promise for developing the kind of ministry the church needs in today's struggling society. The confrontational man-in-charge style currently taught in some church growth seminars and extolled in too much of the current literature has abandoned the reconciliatory servant-leader model of the New Testament.

The secular leadership model shows us a "strong" person whose autocratic drive pushes others before him. But Christian leaders are marked primarily by their difference from the world, not by their adherence to secular models. Biblical leaders share authority with their followers and believe that leadership is primarily ministry to others. That kind of climate invites people to join ministry as genuine team members.

A key factor in Dave's success lay in that behind-the-scenes work when he mapped out his plan and brought in key people to share his goals. Those people were not puppets to make Dave's system work, but participants in a genuine team ministry.

Leadership that Attracts People to Ministry

One of the unique features of most congregations is the makeup of the membership. Some new Christians are excited about the work of the church and want to become involved in its ministry. Others have often already served in positions of leadership. Then there will be new volunteers ready to serve. On the survey (chapter 3) you need to provide a place for all these possible groups to indicate their desires. What better way to discover this kind of information? The church that gives proper planning to the survey process is on the way to developing a ministry team.

In an interesting article entitled "Many Are Called, Few Volunteer" Barbara Bolton reminds us to "explain the framework within which each person is to function."

Everyone needs to know where her or his part of the job fits into the overall scheme of things. Everyone needs to know where to turn for help in clarification.

Some people simply stop working if they become frustrated or confused, so provide them with phone numbers of experienced volunteers, if possible.

If you're chairing a large group, enlist at least two associate chairmen to serve as sounding boards for those who encounter problems. Remember the rule of ten: ideally, each person will have no more than ten others turning to her or him for help.[1]

Just because people volunteer for ministry does not mean they will fit into a ministry team. If there are no positions available, let them know and keep them on the list for future opportunities. If they desire training, let them know when the next training session will be held. If their personalities do not fit well with the other members of an existing ministry team, don't push them into those positions just because there may be a need.

Don't forget how Dave started. He spent the first year behind the scenes getting to know people, considering the issues, and pulling together a team. Effective teams attract new members; ineffective teams repel potential members.

Leadership that Models Ministry for People

Though the members of his team may not have noticed it, Dave began modeling ministry before he ever brought them together. His careful preparation, careful selection of team members and careful arrangement of team relationships modeled a pattern they could follow in the care group ministry to which God had called them. His openness to their suggestions, frustrations, and fears clarified what leadership needs to be. This is precisely how Jesus handled the disciples during the three years they learned team ministry under his leadership. Because of what Dave's team became, and because of what Dave demonstrated as a leader, the members of that group eagerly stayed together rather than finding excuses to abandon the team.

Leadership that Encourages People in Ministry

Sometimes we think it would be more comfortable if church ministry could be carried out exclusively by professionally trained staff members. We could require them to attend meetings, raise their pay when they function well and fire them if they are ineffective. It would save hours not to have to ask people to serve and wait to find out whether or not they will do so.

But there are two major problems to this plan. First, it isn't biblical. The growth of the New Testament church rested clearly on its capacity to draw on lay leaders almost exclusively. The apostle Paul stands out in the Book of Acts precisely because he was so different from everyone else, the "professional clergyman" amid dozens of lay volunteers.

Second, no church can operate without a core of lay volunteers. Pastor Wayne Jacobsen reminds us that lay leaders "aren't as available, but they are better distributed."

> It's tough to get people together. But when I look at ministry as touching people instead of attending meetings, I realize what makes them unavailable for my schedule makes them readily accessible to others. I can be at only one place at a time, dealing with a limited number of people, but my parishioners are spread out all over the city. And whereas I need to schedule an appointment weeks in advance, some lay person will be free to go over tonight and spend hours helping someone. One farmer and his wife found 15 hours in a single week to help a person through a major crisis.[2]

Effective local church programs have always been lay led. When churches buy into the super professionalism of modern society, they may design slick platform operations and in the process lose the interest of people who desperately need to be involved and whose spiritual gifts can contribute significantly to the overall ministry of the congregation.

What Locke Bowman says about Sunday school is appropriate.

If the clergy and other professionals were to decide that Sunday school needed to be renewed, and if they empowered the laity to devote talent and energy to the task, then nothing could stop the renewal from beginning. We wait for articulate pastors and Christian educators to sound the call.[3]

Of course pastoral response to such a proposal depends on philosophy of ministry and leadership. In our opinion, a team approach to church leadership offers the only viable alternative.

Leadership that Understands Biblical Ministry Effectiveness

Perhaps Christians are too deeply enmeshed in the secularization of the society to rethink the whole issue of success and failure. But if they do, they may discover that biblical values are and always have been counterculture. The Scriptures speak to this issue at numerous points, one of which is the dramatic treatise on stewardship in Luke.

"No servant can serve two masters. Either he will hate the one and love the other, or he will be devoted to the one and despise the other. You cannot serve both God and Money." The Pharisees, who loved money, heard all this and were sneering at Jesus. He said to them, "You are the ones who justify yourselves in the eyes of men, but God knows your hearts. What is highly valued among men is detestable in God's sight" (16:13–15).

The second thing to discover is that biblical heroes tended to be worldly failures. Read again through the first ten verses of Hebrews 11. Sense the loneliness of

Enoch and Noah, of the rejected Moses fleeing into the desert abandoned by his noble friends of the Egyptian court, of the outcast Rahab, and of the erratic Jephthah. Of these and others the Bible says, "The world was not worthy of them" and no wonder, since the world scoffs at biblical criteria for success. Church volunteers must understand those criteria: relationships of love (1 Cor. 13:1–3), a servant attitude (Matt. 20:24–28), and faithfulness (Matt. 25:14–21).

Finally, biblical faith transcends temporal applause. Again the Hebrews passage is helpful.

> All these people were still living by faith when they died. They did not receive the things promised; they only saw them and welcomed them from a distance. And they admitted that they were aliens and strangers on earth. People who say such things show that they are looking for a country of their own. If they had been thinking of the country they had left, they would have had opportunity to return. Instead, they were longing for a better country—a heavenly one. Therefore God is not ashamed to be called their God, for he has prepared a city for them (11:13–16).

The world screams for fame and applause, while Dorcas sits quietly mending the garments of the widows at Joppa. The world wants to know how many channels carry your religious program, while Barnabas quietly takes Mark back to Cyprus for long-term one-on-one discipleship training. The world gathers to watch its heroes place hand prints and footprints in the cement of time, while Paul rots in Mamertine Prison asking only for his coat, his writing materials, and the visit of a few remaining faithful friends.

Church leaders will find it extremely difficult to communicate those biblical standards, but it is the only way genuinely spiritual ministry teams can be built.

Team Ministry Requires Effective Nurturing

Nurturing is not a difficult word to understand, especially for gardeners and parents. Plants and children need a special climate, careful watering and feeding, and sometimes pruning. That's the function Dave served with his ministry team and that's the function every team leader carries out if he wants to be effective in that role. We have already emphasized showing appreciation, finding the right place of ministry for each person, helping people get along together, providing adequate resources, and designing peer fellowship groups. All these are basic. In addition, the following suggestions should help you increase your retention ratio within a year.

Nurturing that Creates an Attractive Climate

One of the great churches of the New Testament was founded in Antioch, a city of a half-million people steeped in idolatry and immorality. Significantly larger than Jerusalem, Antioch was the third largest city in the Roman Empire at the time of the first-century church. As we read Acts 11 we immediately sense a positive climate for ministry in that great urban congregation. The church was founded by anonymous Greek-speaking Jews and first pastored by a lay leader named Barnabas sent up from Jerusalem. You will recall that Barnabas was a nickname meaning "son of encouragement." The text in the New Testament says, "When he arrived and saw the evidence of the grace of God, he was glad and encouraged them all to remain true to the Lord with all their hearts" (Acts 11:23).

A ministry climate that retains volunteers is positive, relaxed, and encouraging. It avoids rules and restrictions, unnecessary paper work and meetings, and valueless traditions.

Nurturing that Teaches the Biblical Principle of Service

The essential issue in retention is motivation, not endurance. Some people do just get tired, fatigued in the faith, and drop out. Others get frustrated because of mechanical things like lack of training or inadequate equipment. But many simply don't understand the biblical reasons for serving the Lord. They function from a neurotic compulsion to duty rather than a refreshing joyfulness so obvious among the volunteers of the New Testament.

At Antioch solid Bible teaching was the second component after encouragement.

> Then Barnabas went to Tarsus to look for Saul, and when he found him, he brought him to Antioch. So for a whole year Barnabas and Saul met with the church and taught great numbers of people. The disciples were called Christians first at Antioch (Acts 11:25–26).

Unable to handle the teaching task by himself, Pastor Barnabas went out to find the finest Bible teacher he had ever heard, a young rabbi from Tarsus named Saul. Do not read any retrospective analysis into this choice. When Barnabas made this decision there was no "apostle Paul," only a former persecutor still viewed with suspicion by the Jerusalem church. Doubtless many believers in Jerusalem thought this a risky appointment. But the people in Antioch needed serious, in-depth Bible teaching so they could understand what God expected from them, and in Barnabas' judgment, Saul was best equipped to do that.

Nurturing that Clarifies a Philosophy of Ministry

The four items mentioned right at the beginning of this chapter described a portion of Dave's philosophy of ministry. Coming to this new leadership role with a background in team ministry, he was able to apply basic guidelines that formulated what we call a philosophy of ministry. That is simply a way of describing why we do what we do in the church.

The clarification of a mission statement and objectives lays the foundation for a philosophy of ministry. We need not get too scholarly here. Just write a clear statement about why your church carries out its ministries in the way it does. Why two or three morning services rather than a branch church? Why care groups on Sunday evening rather than another worship service? Why boys' and girls' club programs instead of a centralized youth ministry? Or why both, or neither?

People stay focused in ministry when they see how that ministry fits the larger picture. But they cannot understand that larger picture unless they have a clear handle on your congregational philosophy of ministry. Effective ministry leaders not only understand and write out a philosophy of ministry, they also go over it and over it and over it with volunteer teams.

Philosophy of ministry in your congregation should recognize multiple and diverse models of ministry. Each congregation must ask itself, "Why has God raised up this church in this place at this time, and what does he want from us?" Unless volunteers understand the answers to those questions, they cannot serve effectively on ministry teams.

Nurturing that Strives to Produce New Leaders

Too often people look only at *the leader* herself, her gifts, her talents, and her experience. But leadership is never individual; it always relates to *other people*. One can manage behind the scenes comfortably hidden by paperwork and computer printouts; but one can lead only in the midst of people. So you ask about a potential volunteer not only, How has God gifted him? but also, What can she do to meet the needs of the particular group of people with whom we want her to serve?

There is a third component well documented in the research of leadership: *the situation*. A person effective in one group might not be effective with another. A person effective in one setting might work well in that situation but fail dramatically in another. A good Sunday school teacher might be a poor weekday club director. A person gifted in individual evangelism may not function well in Old Testament exposition. People stay on the job when they understand themselves, the dynamics of the group in which they serve, and the variables of any situation.

At Antioch, Barnabas and Saul represented different types of leaders with very different gifts and personalities. Their group consisted of new converts who did not fit the pattern of historic Judaism that marked the church in Jerusalem. The situation was a pagan urban center renowned for sin in which God, by His providence, had chosen to raise up a vital and dynamic church. These kinds of biblical and sociological factors make a big difference in whether people choose to quit or hang on in their ministry positions.

Team Ministry Requires Effective Relationships

The early paragraphs of this chapter do not exactly spell out what Dave did with his team members to develop relationships. But one of the "pieces of knowledge" he utilized as an effective leader was his understanding of team development and that assumes the building of effective relationships. Those connections run in numerous directions but of greatest importance are relationships between the team unit and the leader, and among all the team members.

Over twenty years ago Roger Gray wrote an interesting article for the *Hillsdale College Leadership Letter*, titled "Generating Co-Operation Is Leading." His major thrust was that the primary evidence of leadership is the ability to generate cooperation among people. Consider this thought: "The leader who is so experienced and so skilled that his observations, his experiments, his judgments, and his communications develop cooperation rather than conflict, is the one most likely to maintain the position of leadership."[4]

Relationships that Minimize Problems of Bureaucracy

Bureaucracy, in our common vocabulary, tends to be a negative concept. But as a technical word it merely describes the intricate way organizations fit together, and, to a greater or lesser extent, all churches have some kind of bureaucracy. But leaders need to understand how to function within the organization, not circumvent it or be frustrated in it. Colossians 3 teaches us clearly that we work for the boss but we ultimately work for Christ. Individual team members cannot decide what is best for the ministry of the church if it goes against what the team leader believes. That does not extol any kind of autocratic attitudes on the part of the leader; it merely means that cooperation with the system is biblical behavior both in secular government (Rom. 13) and in the church.

Team leaders need to represent their ministry supervisors fairly, understand them as much as possible, and keep them informed. Obviously they need to be taught these principles.

Relationships that Nourish Creativity

Creativity comes when we give people credit for making good mistakes. Experimenting with new ways to minister effectively will sometimes lead to failure. But that is good failure which occurs every time people make a serious attempt to challenge the process and improve the system.

Creativity becomes possible when we keep the organization flexible, improve communication among the team members, and don't force conformity on the out-of-step person. That very person, the one who seems to be just a bit different than the other members of the team, may very well be the one with the new ideas that make possible greater team achievements in ministry.

Relationships that Help People Deal With Criticism

Effective team leaders are not afraid of criticism, because they know it's inevitable and being afraid of it is nonproductive. Furthermore, if they have been trained to deal with criticism, they will recognize handling it is a part of any cooperative venture. Several questions are useful here: Does the criticism reflect needs or hurts of the critic? Is the criticism valid? True? Necessary? What might you learn from this criticism?

Relationships that Balance Loyalty in Ministry

Our training programs must balance loyalty in team ministry. The timeless antithesis in the history of management research focuses on the individual versus the organization. For us that means asking whether the volunteer serves the church or the church serves the volunteer. Obviously, both must be in place to keep the balance. Dayton and Engstrom describe the necessity of a careful development program like the team training opportunities discussed in this book.

A Christian organization and its various subcomponents have a responsibility to develop people in their relationship to their Master and toward one another. Discovering ways to make prayer an intimate part of the working life of the company is not easy, but it is essential. Expecting that the staff will have the concern one for another in terms of personal life is difficult, but that's what Christianity is all about. In other words, the Bible calls us to specific corporate acts and attitudes, and we have to find ways to respond to these imperatives.[5]

Remember that a good team leader keeps team members alert to any changes that might affect their ministries. Sometimes that may be a simple announcement about time or equipment. In other cases, however, it could be the necessity for continuing education to upgrade skills and stay effective in the ministry. Everyone needs to be refreshed and recharged from time to time, and short-term training programs can help provide that essential ingredient of ministry.

Dave never forgot that the members of his team made possible whatever ministry effectiveness he enjoyed, and, you will recall, he never failed to give those people credit when someone commented on the effectiveness of the ministry he had been asked to lead. The ministry team is only as good as its leader.

Application Activities

1. What level of satisfaction is there among the team members in your church? Do they feel appreciated? Do they sense the importance of their task? What specifically can you and other church leaders do to demonstrate appreciation to the workers for their faithful ministry?

2. Would you categorize your church as an effective team ministry or as a number of individuals promoting their own programs? People are fulfilled when they consider themselves a vital part of a team ministry. Suggest some possible ways this concept could be facilitated.

3. Are workers in your church motivated by guilt or by a proper understanding of their place in God's service? Evaluate this carefully, as many churches use improper motivational techniques. What are some positive ways to encourage workers to stay with their ministries and do their work effectively?

4. Review the record of Dave's leadership at the beginning of the chapter and at various points throughout. Identify at least ten lessons for developing team ministry that you can find in his example.

5. Name some ways your church nourishes creativity on ministry teams. How do you build in rewards for "good failure"? How do you help people deal with criticism?

Conclusion

D ouglas Johnson put it well a few years ago when he entitled his first book on developing lay leaders *The Care and Feeding of Volunteers.* If we have tended in this book to talk in terms that sound too mechanical—*recruiting, enlisting, training, placing, supervising, evaluating*—it's only because these words describe what we must actually do to build effective ministry teams. But we agree with Johnson; the key to finding and keeping effective volunteers is to nurture them in an environment that helps them grow spiritually and professionally as they carry out the ministries for which God has gifted them.

Furthermore, the recruitment of volunteers should never aim at a ministry maintenance goal. While carrying out the tasks of any given ministry, we want to develop team relationships that build leadership in our volunteers. To do that we must never forget that *leadership development cannot take place unless situation and strength overlap.* That is to say, when we have people with gifts, strengths, and talents in a given ministry, they can never develop leadership unless we place them in that ministry and not one for which they are ill fitted.

When people in any congregation exercise ministry for which God has gifted them through the power of the Holy Spirit, they can, under a caring, nurturing leadership, make exciting things happen. So put words like *duty* and *drudgery* behind you. Stop focusing on maintenance and accept the exciting challenges of the future. Help people find the places God wants them to serve and turn them loose to function effectively in those volunteer ministries.

Bibliography

Church Leadership Development. Glen Ellyn, Ill.: Scripture Press, 1977.

Dibbert, Michael T. *Spiritual Leadership, Responsible Management: A Guide for Leaders of the Church.* Grand Rapids: Zondervan, 1989.

Doohan, Leonard. *Laity's Mission in the Local Church.* San Francisco: Harper & Row, 1986.

————. *Theology and Spirituality.* Minneapolis: Winston, 1984.

Flanagan, Joan. *The Successful Volunteer Organization.* 1981.

Gangel, Kenneth O. *Feeding and Leading.* Wheaton: Victor, 1989.

Gangel, Kenneth O., and Samuel L. Canine. *Communication and Conflict Management in Churches and Christian Organizations.* Nashville: Broadman, 1993.

Henricksen, Walter A. *Disciples Are Made Not Born.* Wheaton: Victor, 1988.

Johnson, Douglas W. *The Care and Feeding of Volunteers.* Creative Leadership Series, ed. Lyle E. Schaller. Nashville: Abingdon, 1978.

———. *Empowering Lay Volunteers*. Creative Leadership Series, ed. Lyle E. Schaller. Nashville: Abingdon, 1991.

Lawrence, William D. *Developing Lay Leadership*. Dallas Theological Seminary: Continuing Education Seminar.

Mason, David E. *Voluntary Non-Profit Enterprise Management*. New York: Plenum, 1984.

Maves, Paul B. *Older Volunteers in Church and Community*, 1981.

Messner, Robert C. *Leadership Development Through S.E.R.V.I.C.E.* Cincinnati: Standard, 1989.

Patterson, Richard. *Effectively Leading; A Guide for All Church Leaders*. Wheaton: Evangelical Training Association, 1992.

Ratcliff, Donald, and Blake J. Neff. *The Complete Guide to Religious Education Volunteers*. Birmingham: Religious Education Press, 1992.

Senter, Mark. *The Art of Recruiting Volunteers*. Wheaton: Victor, 1983.

———. *Recruiting Volunteers in the Church: Resolve Your Recruiting Hassles*. Wheaton: Victor, 1990.

Shelley, Bruce, and Marshall Shelley. *Consumer Church*. Downers Grove, Ill.: InterVarsity, 1992.

Stevens, R. Paul. *Liberating the Laity: Equipping All the Saints for Ministry*. Downers Grove, Ill.: InterVarsity, 1985.

Ver Straten, Charles A. *How to Start Lay-Shepherding Ministries*. Grand Rapids: Baker, 1983.

Walz, Edgar. *How to Manage Your Church*. St. Louis: Concordia, 1987.

Wedel, Leonard E. *Building and Maintaining a Church Staff*. Nashville: Broadman, 1966.

Westing, Harold J. *Evaluate & Grow: Steps to a More Effective Sunday School*. Wheaton: Victor, 1984.

———. *Multiple Church Staff Handbook*. Grand Rapids: Kregel, 1985.

Wilson, Marlene. *How to Mobilize Church Volunteers*. Minneapolis: Augsburg, 1983.

Wortley, Judy. *The Recruiting Remedy: Taking the Headache Out of Finding Volunteers*. Elgin, Ill.: David C. Cook, 1990.

Notes

Introduction

1. Beth E. Brown and Dennis E. Williams, *Christian Education Field Survey* (Denver: Denver Seminary, 1988), 4.

Chapter 1

1. R. Paul Stevens, *Liberating the Laity: Equipping All the Saints for Ministry* (Downers Grove, Ill.: InterVarsity, 1985), 36.
2. George Barna, *User Friendly Churches* (Ventura, Calif.: Regal, 1991), 162.
3. George H. Gallup, Jr., PRRC *Emerging Trends* (October 1992): 14:8:2.
4. Ted W. Engstrom, Edward R. Dayton, eds., *Christian Leadership Letter* (World Vision. March 1987): 1–2.

Chapter 2

1. Eugene B. Habecker, *Leading With a Follower's Heart* (Wheaton: Victor, 1990), 29.
2. Ibid., 30–32.

3. Ibid., 33.
4. R. Paul Stevens, *Liberating the Laity: Equipping All the Saints for Ministry* (Downers Grove, Ill.: InterVarsity, 1985), 34.
5. Lawrence O. Richards and Clyde Hoeldtke, *A Theology of Church Leadership* (Grand Rapids: Zondervan, 1980), 115.
6. Kenneth O. Gangel, "Biblical Theology of Leadership," *Christian Education Journal* (Autumn 1991): XII: 1: 28–29.
7. Eugene H. Peterson, *The Contemplative Pastor: Returning to the Art of Spiritual Direction* (Carol Stream, Ill.: The Leadership Library, Christianity Today, Inc., and Dallas: Word, 1989), 69–70.
8. George Barna, *User Friendly Churches* (Ventura, Calif.: Regal, 1991), 144.
9. Marlene Wilson, *How to Mobilize Church Volunteers* (Minneapolis: Augsburg House, 1983), 21.
10. Barna, 34.

Chapter 3

1. Adapted from Galilee Baptist Church, Denver, 1991.
2. Marlene Wilson, *How to Mobilize Church Volunteers* (Minneapolis: Augsburg House, 1983), 22.
3. Ibid., 41.
4. Vern Heidebrecht, "Affirming the Laity for Ministry," *Direction* (Fall 1990) 19: 2: 45.
5. David L. Rambo, "Every Pastor a Gift Prospector," *Briefing* (Colorado Springs: The Christian and Missionary Alliance, April 1992): 2.

Chapter 4

1. Marlene Wilson, *How to Mobilize Church Volunteers* (Minneapolis: Augsburg House, 1983), 35.
2. Douglas W. Johnson, *Empowering Lay Volunteers; Creative Leadership Series,* Lyle E. Schaller, ed. (Nashville: Abingdon, 1991), 96–97.
3. Johnson, 36.
4. George Barna, *User Friendly Churches* (Ventura, Calif.: Regal, 1991), 163.
5. Carl George, "Recruitment's Missing Link," *Leadership* (Fall 1982): 58–59.

Chapter 5

1. Eugene H. Peterson, *The Contemplative Pastor* (Dallas: Word, 1989), 119.
2. Bruce P. Powers, *Church Administration Handbook* (Nashville: Broadman, 1985), 70.
3. John R. Cionca, *The Trouble Shooting Guide To Christian Education* (Denver: Accent, 1986), 9.
4. W. Steven Brown, *13 Fatal Errors Managers Make and How You Can Avoid Them* (New York: Berkley, 1987), 22.
5. *Royal Bank of Canada Monthly Letter* (July 1977): 58: 7: 2.
6. *Church Growth Research News* (Winter 1985): 4.

Chapter 6

1. Edward R. Dayton and Ted W. Engstrom, *Strategy for Leadership: Planning, Activating, Motivating* (Old Tappan, N.J.: Revell, 1979), 39.
2. Mary Walton, *The Deming Management Method* (New York: Perigee Books, Putnam, 1986), 34–36.

3. Paul G. Hiebert, "Training Leaders, Training Followers." *Theology, News and Notes* (June 1989) : 36: 2: 23.
4. Fred R. Wilson, "Why Church Volunteers Attend Religious Training Programs," *Christian Education Journal* (Spring 1992) : XII: 3: 82.
5. Ronald G. Held, "How to Develop Qualified Workers," *Ministries* (Spring 1984) : 2: 2: 53.

Chapter 7

1. Ted Engstrom and Ed Dayton, "Competence," *Christian Leadership Letter* (August 1981): 3.

Chapter 8

1. Barbara Weeks Bolton, "Many Are Called, Few Volunteer," *Today's Christian Woman* (July/ August 1987): 42.
2. Pastor Wayne Jacobsen, "Five Reasons Not to Equip Lay People," *Leadership* (Summer 1988): 49.
3. Locke Bowman, Jr., "The General Protestant Sunday School." *Renewing the Sunday School and the CCD*, D. Campbell Wyckoff, ed. (Birmingham, Ala.: 1986), 110.
4. Roger Gray, "Generating Co-Operation Is Leading." *Hillsdale College Leadership Letter*, (1971): 10:3.
5. Ed Dayton and Ted Engstrom, "Developing and Training Staff," *Christian Leadership Letter* (April 1980): 3.